SYMBOL, STATUS, AND PERSONALITY

Le Roi Matthew - Pierre Smith

Other books by S. I. Hayakawa

OLIVER WENDELL HOLMES: *Representative Selections,*

with Introduction, Bibliography, and Notes

LANGUAGE IN ACTION

LANGUAGE IN THOUGHT AND ACTION

LANGUAGE, MEANING, AND MATURITY, *editor*

OUR LANGUAGE AND OUR WORLD, *editor*

THE USE AND MISUSE OF LANGUAGE, *editor*

SYMBOL,

STATUS, AND

PERSONALITY

S. I. Hayakawa

A HARVEST BOOK

HARCOURT, BRACE & WORLD, INC.

New York

Library of Congress Catalog Card Number: 63-17772

Some of these essays previously appeared, a number in slightly different form, in the following publications: *Common Sense, Etc., Journal of Dental Medicine, The Reconstructionist, The Saturday Evening Post, trans/formation, and Western Reserve Law Review.*

Printed in the United States of America

G.6.69

FOREWORD

The essays in this volume all reflect, to greater or lesser degree, the influence of the general semantics of Alfred Korzybski (1879-1950), a system of thought that continues, after twenty-five years of acquaintance with it, to prove useful and fascinating to me. The central concern of general semantics is to understand symbolism, including language—and to understand how symbolism is both used and abused.

"Meaning . . . characterizes symbolism," says Dr. Frederick Hacker, "and the objective phenomenon of 'symbol' has its subjective counterpart in the experience of 'meaning.' . . . Every insight into meaning, what it consists of, how it is produced, how it can be manipulated, is implicitly a contribution to action psychology. The logical and psychological aspects of meaning are always jointly present. . . . In symbols the idiosyncratic and personal are always intermingled with the general and universal. Precisely this interplay constitutes symbols and prescribes meaning. . . . Not only does the human being use and create symbols, but the individual is also made and created by symbolism."

General semantics, then, is the study of what makes human beings human. Moreover, in its inquiry into the disorders of symbolism, whether these take the form of nationalistic madness, footless political and religious controversy, superstition, or mental illness, general semantics is also the study of what makes human beings sometimes less than human.

Since symbols are necessary to science as well as to art, and since symbolic considerations enter into almost everything human beings concern themselves with—food, clothing, housing, amusement, work, fighting, ceremony, and religion—the student of general semantics finds it difficult to confine himself to one field of knowledge, to one academic specialty. Every symbolic event—the make-believe play of children, a toothpaste jingle on the radio, the laying of a wreath at the grave of a national hero, the overthrow of one theory about atomic particles by another, the self-immolation of a Buddhist priest in Vietnam, a protest march in Washington—is as likely as not to arouse reflection and speculation on the part of the general semanticist.

The fact that there are no discernible limits to the study of language and symbolism has its dangers as well as its advantages. The principal danger, of course, is the temptation to carry his speculations into fields in which he is no expert. I am afraid the dangers are revealed all too clearly in this volume. I hope, however, that some of the advantages are also revealed. Whatever the dangers of trying to encompass the sciences and the arts and the problems of daily living in a single methodological outlook, a concern with symbolism appears to me a necessary starting point for anyone who would try to unite what C. P. Snow has called the "two cultures."

There are practical implications to general semantics, too. In thinking about human beings and their interaction with each

FOREWORD

other—in the family, in business, in education, in race relations, in therapy—nothing is so important as having at one's fingertips a method of guarding against the pitfalls of language. Words give an aura of permanence and stability to fleeting events. They give the illusion of substance to shadows. With words we unite things that are forever separate, and separate that which is indivisible.

Discourse in the physical sciences has pitfalls enough, but in the main their vocabularies are reasonably well agreed upon. A background of common training unites chemists, for example, in their understanding of such words as "amino acids" or "polymerization" or "colloid." But in the language of everyday life, and to a considerable degree in the languages of the social sciences, such common understandings cannot be assumed. Even to talk to ourselves in such terms as "discipline," "basic education," "executive function," "democratic process," or "neurotic personality" is to strew our intellectual course with land mines—unless we train ourselves to ask constantly what the words stand for, if anything, at the time we are using them. Just as a spear-fisherman must make allowances for the way in which water distorts his vision, so must the student of human affairs be aware of the degree to which the language he speaks pulls reality out of shape.

The study of general semantics should have the effect, then, of heightening our awareness of the problems of language and also heightening our awareness of the complexity of the nonverbal realities which language more or less adequately codifies. The shortcomings of this volume are not the shortcomings of general semantics as a method of thought. They are the shortcomings of the author, who still has a long way to go in applying general semantics to the discipline and liberation of his own mind.

San Francisco State College   S. I. HAYAKAWA

vii

CONTENTS

SYMBOL, STATUS, AND PERSONALITY

HOW WORDS CHANGE OUR LIVES

THE end product of education, yours and mine and everybody's, is the total pattern of reactions and possible reactions we have inside ourselves. If you did not have within you at this moment the pattern of reactions that we call "the ability to read English," you would see here only meaningless black marks on paper. Because of the trained patterns of response, you are (or are not) stirred to patriotism by martial music, your feelings of reverence are aroused by the symbols of your religion, you listen more respectfully to the health advice of someone who has "M.D." after his name than to that of someone who hasn't. What I call here a "pattern of reactions," then, is the sum total of the ways we act in response to events, to words, and to symbols.

Our reaction patterns—our semantic habits, as we may call them—are the internal and most important residue of whatever years of education or miseducation we may have received from our parents' conduct toward us in childhood as well as their teachings, from the formal education we may have had, from all the sermons and lectures we have listened to, from the radio programs and the movies and television shows we have experienced, from all the books and newspapers and comic strips we have read, from the conversations we have had with friends and associates, and from all our experiences. If, as the result of all these influences that make us what we are, our semantic habits are reasonably similar to those of most people around us, we are regarded as "well-adjusted," or "normal," and perhaps "dull." If our semantic habits are noticeably different from those of others, we are regarded as "individualistic" or "original," or, if the differences are disapproved of or viewed with alarm, as "screwballs" or "crazy."

Semantics is sometimes defined in dictionaries as "the science of the meaning of words"—which would not be a bad definition if people didn't assume that the search for the meanings of words begins and ends with looking them up in a dictionary.

If one stops to think for a moment, it is clear that to define a word, as a dictionary does, is simply to explain the word with more words. To be thorough about defining, we should next have to define the words used in the definition, then define the words used in defining the words used in the definition . . . and so on. Defining words with more words, in short, gets us at once into what mathematicians call an "infinite regress." Alternatively, it can get us into the kind of run-around we sometimes encounter when we look up "impertinence" and find it defined as "impudence," so we look up "impudence" and find it defined as "impertinence." Yet—and here we come to another common reaction pattern—people often act as if words can be explained fully with more words. To a person who asked for a definition of jazz, Louis Armstrong is said to have replied, "Man, when you got to ask what it is, you'll never get to know," proving himself to be an intuitive semanticist as well as a great trumpet player.

Semantics, then, does not deal with the "meaning of words" as that expression is commonly understood. P. W. Bridgman, the Nobel Prize winner and physicist, once wrote, "The true meaning of a term is to be found by observing what a man does with it, not by what he says about it." He made an enormous contribution to science by showing that the meaning of a scientific term lies in the operations, the things done, that establish its validity, rather than in verbal definitions.

Here is a simple, everyday kind of example of "operational" definition. If you say, "This table measures six feet in length," you could prove it by taking a foot rule, performing the operation of laying it end to end while counting, "One . . . two . . . three . . . four. . . ." But if you say—and revolutionists have started uprisings with just this statement— "Man is born free, but everywhere he is in chains!"—what operations could you perform to demonstrate its accuracy or inaccuracy?

But let us carry this suggestion of "operationalism" outside the physical sciences where Bridgman applied it, and observe what "operations" people perform as the result of both the language they use and the language other people use in communicating to them. Here is a personnel manager studying an application blank. He comes to the words "Education: Harvard University," and drops the application blank in the wastebasket (that's the "operation") because, as he would say if you asked him, "I don't like Harvard men." This is an instance of "meaning" at work—but it is not a meaning that can be found in dictionaries.

If I seem to be taking a long time to explain what semantics is about, it is because I am trying, in the course of explanation, to introduce the reader to a certain way of looking at human behavior. Semantics—especially the general semantics of Alfred Korzybski (1879-1950), Polish-American scientist and educator—pays particular attention not to words in themselves, but to semantic reactions—that is, human responses to symbols, signs, and symbol-systems, including language.

I say *human* responses because, so far as we know, human beings are the only creatures that have, over and above that biological equipment which we have in common with other creatures, the additional capacity for manufacturing symbols and systems of symbols. When we react to a flag, we are not reacting simply to a piece of cloth, but to the meaning with which it has been symbolically endowed. When we react to a word, we are not reacting to a set of sounds, but to the meaning with which that set of sounds has been symbolically endowed.

A basic idea in general semantics, therefore, is that the meaning of words (or other symbols) is not in the words, but in our own semantic reactions. If I were to tell a shockingly obscene story in Arabic or Hindustani or Swahili before an audience that understood only English, no one would blush or be angry; the story would be neither shocking nor obscene—indeed, it would not even be a story. Likewise, the value of a dollar bill is not in the bill, but in our social agreement to accept it as a symbol of value. If that agreement were to break down through the collapse of our government, the dollar bill would become only a scrap of paper. We do not understand a dollar bill by staring at it long and hard. We understand it by observing how people act with respect to it. We understand it by understanding the social mechanisms and the loyalties that keep it meaningful. Semantics is therefore a social study, basic to all other social studies.

It is often remarked that words are tricky—and that we are all prone to be deceived by "fast talkers," such as high-pressure salesmen, skillful propagandists, politicians, or lawyers. Since few of us are aware of the degree to which we use words to deceive ourselves, the sin of "using words in a tricky way" is one that is always attributed to the other fellow. When the Russians use the word "democracy" to mean something quite different from what we mean by it, we at once accuse them of "propaganda," of "corrupting the meanings of words." But when we use the word "democracy" in the United States to mean something quite different from what the Russians mean by it, they are equally quick to accuse us of "hypocrisy." We all tend to believe that the way we use words is the correct way, and that people who use the same words in other ways are either ignorant or dishonest.

Leaving aside for a moment such abstract and difficult terms as "democracy," let us examine a common, everyday word like "frog." Surely there is no problem about what "frog" means! Here are some sample sentences:

"If we're going fishing, we'll have to catch some frogs first." (This is easy.)

"I have a frog in my throat." (You can hear it croaking.)

"She wore a loose silk jacket fastened with braided frogs."

"The blacksmith pared down the frog and the hoof before shoeing the horse."

"In Hamilton, Ohio, there is a firm by the name of American Frog and Switch Company."

In addition to these "frogs," there is the frog in which a sword is carried, the frog at the bottom of a bowl or vase that is used in flower arrangement, and the frog that is part of a violin bow. The reader can no doubt think of other "frogs."

Or take another common word such as "order." There is the *order* that the salesman tries to get, which is quite different from the *order* that a captain gives to his crew. Some people enter holy *orders*. There is the *order* in the house when

7

mother has finished tidying up; there is the batting *order* of the home team; there is an *order* of ham and eggs. It is surprising that with so many meanings to the word, people don't misunderstand one another oftener than they do.

The foregoing are only striking examples of a principle to which we are all so well accustomed that we rarely think of it; namely, that most words have more meanings than dictionaries can keep track of. And when we consider further that each of us has different experiences, different memories, different likes and dislikes, it is clear that all words evoke different responses in all of us. We may agree as to what the term "Mississippi River" stands for, but you and I recall different parts of the river; you and I have had different experiences with it; one of us has read more about it than the other; one of us may have happy memories of it, while the other may recall chiefly tragic events connected with it. Hence your "Mississippi River" can never be identical with my "Mississippi River." The fact that we can communicate with each other about the "Mississippi River" often conceals the fact that we are talking about two different sets of memories and experiences.

Words being as varied in their meanings as they are, no one can tell us what the correct interpretation of a word should be in advance of our next encounter with that word. The reader may have been taught always to revere the word "mother." But what is he going to do the next time he encounters this word, when it occurs in the sentence "Mother began to form in the bottle"? If it is impossible to determine what a single word will mean on next encounter, is it possible to say in advance what is the correct evaluation of such events as these: (1) next summer, an individual who calls himself a socialist will announce his candidacy for the office of register of deeds in your city; (2) next autumn, there will be a strike at one of your local department stores; (3) next week, your wife will announce that she is going to change her style of hairdo; (4) tomorrow, your little boy will come home with a bleeding nose?

A reasonably sane individual will react to each of these events in his own way, according to time, place, and the entire surrounding set of circumstances; and included among those circumstances will be his own stock of experiences, wishes, hopes, and fears. But there are people whose pattern of reactions is such that some of them can be completely predicted in advance. Mr. A will never vote for anyone called "socialist," no matter how incompetent or crooked the alternative candidates may be. Mr. B_1 always disapproves of strikes and strikers, without bothering to inquire whether or not this strike has its justifications; Mr. B_2 always sympathizes with the strikers because he hates all bosses. Mr. C belongs to the "stay sweet as you are" school of thought, so that his wife hasn't been able to change her hairdo since she left high school. Mr. D always faints at the sight of blood.

Such fixed and unalterable patterns of reaction—in their more obvious forms we call them prejudices—are almost inevitably organized around words. Mr. E distrusts and fears all people to whom the term "Catholic" is applicable, while Mr. F, who is Catholic, distrusts and fears all non-Catholics. Mr. G is so rabid a Republican that he reacts with equal dislike to all Democrats, all Democratic proposals, all opposite proposals if they are also made by Democrats. Back in the days when Franklin D. Roosevelt was President, Mr. G disliked not only the Democratic President but also his wife, children, and dog. His office was on Roosevelt Road in Chicago (it had been named after Theodore Roosevelt), but he had his address changed to his back door on 11th Street, so that he would not have to print the hated name on his stationery. Mr. H, on the other hand, is an equally rabid Democrat, who gave up golf during the Eisenhower administration (he resumed it after

Kennedy took up the game). People suffering from such prejudices seem to have in their brains an uninsulated spot which,
when touched by such words as "capitalist," "boss," "striker,"
"scab," "Democrat," "Republican," "socialized medicine," and
other such loaded terms, results in an immediate short circuit,
often with a blowing of fuses.

Korzybski called such short-circuited responses "identification reactions." He used the word "identification" in a
special sense; he meant that persons given to such fixed patterns of response identify (that is, treat as identical all oc-
currences of a given word or symbol; they identify all the different cases that fall under the same name. Thus, if one has
hostile identification reactions to "women drivers," then all
women who drive cars are "identical" in their incompetence.

Korzybski believed that the term "identification reaction"
could be generally used to describe the majority of cases of
semantic malfunctioning. Identification is something that goes
on in the human nervous system. "Out there" there are no absolute identities. No two Harvard men, no two Ford cars, no
two mothers-in-law, no two politicians, no two leaves from the
same tree are identical with each other in all respects. If, however, we treat all cases that fall under the same class label as
one at times when the differences are important, then there is
something wrong with our semantic habits.

We are now ready, then, for another definition of general
semantics. It is a comparative study of the kinds of responses
people make to the symbols and signs around them; we may
compare the semantic habits common among the prejudiced,
the foolish, and the mentally ill with those found among people who are able to solve their problems successfully, so that,
if we care to, we may revise our own semantic habits for the
better. In other words, general semantics is the study of how
not to be a damn fool.

Identification reactions run all the way through nature.

The capacity for seeing similarities is necessary to the survival of all animals. The pickerel, I suppose, identifies all shiny, fluttery things going through the water as minnows, and goes after them all in pretty much the same way. Under natural conditions, life is made possible for the pickerel by this capacity. Once in a while, however, the shiny, fluttery thing in the water may happen to be not a minnow but an artificial lure on the end of a line. In such a case, one would say that the identification response, so useful for survival, under somewhat more complex conditions that require differentiation between two sorts of shiny and fluttery objects, proves to be fatal.

To go back to our discussion of human behavior, we see at once that the problem of adequate differentiation is immeasurably more complex for men than it is for the pickerel. The signs we respond to, and the symbols we create and train ourselves to respond to, are infinitely greater in number and immeasurably more abstract than the signs in a pickerel's environment. Lower animals have to deal only with certain brute facts in their physical environment. But think, only for a moment, of what constitutes a human environment. Think of the items that call for adequate responses that no animal ever has to think about: our days are named and numbered, so that we have birthdays, anniversaries, holidays, centennials, and so on, all calling for specifically human responses; we have history, which no animal has to worry about; we have verbally codified patterns of behavior which we call law, religion, and ethics. We have to respond not only to events in our immediate environment, but to reported events in Washington, Paris, Tokyo, Moscow, Beirut. We have literature, comic strips, confession magazines, market quotations, detective stories, journals of abnormal psychology, bookkeeping systems to interpret. We have money, credit, banking, stocks, bonds, checks, bills. We have the complex symbolisms of moving pictures, paintings, drama, music, architecture, and dress. In short, we live in a vast human dimension of which the lower animals have no inkling, and we have to have a capacity for differentiation adequate to the complexity of our extra environment.

The next question, then, is why human beings do not always have an adequate capacity for differentiation. Why are we not constantly on the lookout for differences as well as similarities instead of feeling, as so many do, that the Chinese (or Mexicans, or ballplayers, or women drivers) are "all alike"? Why do some people react to words as if they were the things they stand for? Why do certain patterns of reaction, both in individuals and in larger groups such as nations, persist long after the usefulness has expired?

Part of our identification reactions are simply protective mechanisms inherited from the necessities of survival under earlier and more primitive conditions of life. I was once beaten up and robbed by two men on a dark street. Months later, I was again on a dark street with two men, good friends of mine, but involuntarily I found myself in a panic and insisted on our hurrying to a well-lighted drugstore to have a soda so that I would stop being jittery. In other words, my whole body responded with an identification reaction of fear of these two men, in spite of the fact that I "knew" that I was in no danger. Fortunately, with the passage of time, this reaction has died away. But the hurtful experiences of early childhood do not fade so readily. There is no doubt that many identification reactions are traceable to childhood traumas, as psychiatrists have shown.

Further identification reactions are caused by communal patterns of behavior which were necessary or thought necessary at one stage or another in the development of a tribe or nation. General directives such as "Kill all snakes," "Never kill cows, which are sacred animals," "Shoot all strangers on sight," "Fall down flat on your face before all members of the aristocracy," or, to come to more modern instances, "Never vote for a Republican," "Oppose all government regulation of business," "Never associate with Negroes on terms of equality," are an enormous factor in the creation of identification reactions.

Some human beings—possibly in their private feelings a majority—can accept these directives in a *human* way: that is, it will not be impossible for them under a sufficiently changed set of circumstances to kill a cow, or not to bow down before an aristocrat, to vote for a Republican, or to accept a Negro as a classmate. Others, however, get these directives so deeply ground into their nervous systems that they become incapable of changing their responses no matter how greatly the circumstances may have changed. Still others, although capable of changing their responses, dare not do so for fear of public opinion. Social progress usually requires the breaking up of these absolute identifications, which often make necessary changes impossible. Society must obviously have patterns of behavior; human beings must obviously have habits. But when those patterns become inflexible, so that a tribe has only one way to meet a famine, namely, to throw more infants as sacrifices to the crocodiles, or a nation has only one way to meet a threat to its security, namely, to increase its armaments, then such a tribe or such a nation is headed for trouble. There is insufficient capacity for differentiated behavior.

Furthermore—and here one must touch upon the role of newspapers, radio, and television—if agencies of mass communication hammer away incessantly at the production of, let us say, a hostile set of reactions at such words as "Communists," "bureaucrats," "Wall Street," "international bankers," "labor leaders," and so on, no matter how useful an immediate job they may perform in correcting a given abuse at a given time and place, they can in the long run produce in thousands of readers and listeners identification reactions to the words

—reactions that will make intelligent public discussion impossible. Modern means of mass communication and propaganda certainly have an important part to play in the creation of identification reactions.

In addition to the foregoing, there is still another source of identification reactions; namely, the language we use in our daily thought and speech. Unlike the languages of the sciences, which are carefully constructed, tailor-made, special-purpose languages, the language of everyday life is one directly inherited and haphazardly developed from those of our prescientific ancestors: primitive Indo-Europeans, primitive Germanic tribes, Anglo-Saxons. With their scant knowledge of the world, they formulated descriptions of the world before them in statements such as "The sun rises." We do not today believe that the sun "rises." Nevertheless, we still continue to use the expression, without believing what we say.

But there are other expressions, quite as primitive as the idea of "sunrise," which we use uncritically, fully believing in the implications of our terms. Having observed (or heard) that *some* Negroes are lazy, an individual may say, making a huge jump beyond the known facts, "Negroes are lazy." Without arguing for the moment the truth or falsity of this statement, let us examine the implications of the statement as it is ordinarily constructed: "Negroes are lazy." The statement implies, as common sense or any textbook on traditional logic will tell us, that "laziness" is a "quality" that is "inherent" in Negroes.

What are the facts? Under conditions of slavery, under which Negroes were not paid for working, there wasn't any point in being an industrious and responsible worker. The distinguished French abstract artist Jean Hélion once told the story of his life as a prisoner of war in a German camp, where, during World War II, he was compelled to do forced labor. He told how he loafed on the job, how he thought of device after

14

device for avoiding work and producing as little as possible—
and, since his prison camp was a farm, how he stole chickens
at every opportunity. He also described how he put on an
expression of good-natured imbecility whenever approached
by his Nazi overseers. Without intending to do so, in describing his own actions, he gave an almost perfect picture of the
literary type of the Southern Negro of slavery days. Jean
Hélion, confronted with the fact of forced labor, reacted as intelligently as Southern Negro slaves, and the slaves reacted as
intelligently as Jean Hélion. "Laziness," then, is not an "inherent quality" of Negroes or of any other group of people. It
is a *response* to a work situation in which there are no re-
wards for working, and in which one hates his taskmasters.

Statements implying inherent qualities, such as "Negroes
are lazy" or "There's something terribly wrong with young
people today," are therefore the crudest kind of unscientific
observation, based on an out-of-date way of saying things, like
"The sun rises." The tragedy is not simply the fact that people make such statements; the graver fact is that they believe
themselves.

Some individuals are admired for their "realism" because, as the saying goes, they "call a spade a spade." Suppose
we were to raise the question "Why should anyone call it a
spade?" The reply would obviously be, "Because that's what
it is!" This reply appeals so strongly to the common sense of
most people that they feel that at this point discussion can be
closed. I should like to ask the reader, however, to consider a
point which may appear at first to him a mere quibble.

Here, let us say, is an implement for digging made of
steel, with a wooden handle. Here, on the other hand, is a succession of sounds made with the tongue, lips, and vocal cords:
"spade." If you want a digging implement of the kind we are
talking about, you would ask for it by making the succession
of sounds "spade" if you are addressing an English-speaking

person. But suppose you were addressing a speaker of Dutch, French, Hungarian, Chinese, Tagalog? Would you not have to make completely different sounds? It is apparent, then, that the common-sense opinion of most people, "We call a spade a spade because that's what it is," is completely and utterly wrong. We call it a "spade" because we are English-speaking people conforming, in this instance, to majority usage in naming this particular object. The steel-and-iron digging implement is simply an object standing there against the garage door; "spade" is what we *call* it—"spade" is a *name*.

And here we come to another source of identification reactions—an unconscious assumption about language epitomized in the expression "a spade is a spade," or even more elegantly in the famous remark "Pigs are called pigs because they are such dirty animals." The assumption is that everything has a "right name" and that the "right name" names the "essence" of that which is named.

If this assumption is at work in our reaction patterns, we are likely to be given to premature and often extremely inappropriate responses. We are likely to react to names as if they gave complete insight into the persons, things, or situations named. In spite of the fact that my entire education has been in Canada and the United States and I am unable to read and write Japanese, I am sometimes credited with, or accused of, having an "Oriental mind." Now, since Buddha, Confucius, General Tojo, Mao Tse-tung, Syngman Rhee, Pandit Nehru, and the proprietor of the Golden Pheasant Chop Suey House all have "Oriental minds," it is hard to imagine what is meant. The "Oriental mind," like the attribute of "Jewishness," is purely and simply a fiction. Nevertheless, I used to note with alarm that newspaper columnists got paid for articles that purported to account for Stalin's behavior by pointing out that since he came from Georgia, which is next to Turkey and Azerbaijan and therefore "more a part of Asia than of Europe," he too had an "Oriental mind."

To realize fully the difference between words and what they stand for is to be ready for differences as well as similarities in the world. This readiness is mandatory to scientific thinking, as well as to sane thinking. Korzybski's simple but powerful suggestion is to add "index numbers" to all terms, according to the formula: A_1 is not A_2; it can be translated as follows: Cow_1 is not cow_2; cow_2 is not cow_3; politician$_1$ is not politician$_2$; ham and eggs (Plaza Hotel) are not ham and eggs (Smitty's Café); socialism (Russia) is not socialism (England); private enterprise (Joe's Shoe Repair Shop) is not private enterprise (A.T.&T.).

This device of "indexing" will not automatically make us wiser and better, but it's a start. When we talk or write, the habit of indexing our general terms will reduce our tendency to wild and woolly generalization. It will compel us to think before we speak—think in terms of concrete objects and events and situations, rather than in terms of verbal associations. When we read or listen, the habit of indexing will help us visualize more concretely, and therefore understand better, what is being said. And if nothing is being said except deceptive windbaggery, the habit of indexing may—at least part of the time—save us from snapping, like the pickerel, at phony minnows. Another way of summing up is to remember, as Wendell Johnson said, that "To a mouse, cheese is cheese— that's why mousetraps work."

THE TYRANNY OF WORDS

STUDENTS of general semantics are often derided for the emphasis they place on the rule that "the word is not the thing." "Everyone," their critics say scornfully, "knows that!" One can only reply, "The hell they do!" Of course, everyone *says* he knows the difference between words and things. But instead of listening to what people say, let us notice how they act.

Recently a superintendent of public instruction of the State of California started a campaign to drive from high-school libraries throughout the state a certain plain-spoken dictionary on the ground that it contained definitions of obscene words. Students must be protected from such influences, it was argued, because knowledge of evil—in this case knowledge of words having to do with forbidden sexual behavior—would incite evil. To imagine that the mere knowledge of words can be the cause of behavior described by those words is certainly to subscribe to word-magic no less primitive than the belief that one must never talk about death, because death will surely result. This is one example of what general semanticists mean when they say that people often confuse words and things.

In matters of race and nationality, people are especially prone to treat words as things. At a reception I once attended, I saw a tall young American woman with light-brown hair, peaches-and-cream complexion, obviously "Nordic," being introduced as "Mrs. Sakamoto." Her husband was Japanese. The gentleman to whom she was being introduced, a professor and a Ph.D., apparently heard the name but wasn't sure he could repeat it. "Will you please say your name again for me slowly?" he said. "I find your names extremely difficult. I suppose you find our names difficult too. My name is Harrison." In other words, "Mrs. Sakamoto" being a Japanese *name,* he thought of her as a Japanese *person,* although it would have been difficult to imagine anyone less Japanese-looking than she.

Notice, too, the reality that the word "Negro" has for many white people. For some, this word produces so many semantic disturbances that rational thought immediately becomes impossible. Indeed, the inability of most people to think clearly and dispassionately about Negroes constitutes in itself one of the gravest problems confronting the United States. It is useless to point out that, if we in American regard as Negroes all who are part Negro, it would be just as logical to regard as white all who are part white. Many people will simply stare at you angrily and say, "We don't *regard* part Negroes as Negroes. They *are* Negroes!" For many people, the word "Negro" is indeed a "thing."

Treating words as things is a tradition of long standing in our culture. Underlying it is an ancient "philosophical tradition," stemming from a number of notions held by the ancient

Greeks and formalized by their philosophers. Languages are enormous systems of classification made possible by the fact that human nervous systems are capable of abstracting data from experience and generalizing. Were we incapable of abstracting and generalizing, and symbolizing those abstractions with words, experience would be a meaningless and chaotic mess. But languages are made by men, and different men who have different purposes and backgrounds evolve different ways of abstracting. The Greeks, who were in linguistic matters naïve and provincial, made the error common to the linguistically naïve of all times and places: they believed that their own way of abstracting and classifying the events of experience was the only possible way; they believed that in abstracting and classifying as they did, they were following the dictates of "nature" or an objectified "reason," rather than the dictates of their inherited language.

"For one who knows no language but his own," said the late Professor Warner Fite, "the correspondence of words and things is an assumption almost inevitable. For him then the words are not merely conventional symbols for things but real properties of things. . . . It is then a disillusionment to discover, upon learning a foreign language, that what can be expressed in a word in one tongue requires a pair of words or a whole phrase in another, and that between no two languages is there more than a rather loose correspondence of word to word. This wrenches the word loose from the thing; it also introduces what is for me the most characteristic product of philosophical reflection; namely, a consciousness of the variety of human points of view. And the fact that this consciousness is slight in ancient philosophy, acute in all the modern period, may be traced, I think, to the fact that the modern philosopher lives in a world of many tongues, where the Greek philosophers knew only one. And I will go a step further and suggest that this experience of language which the ancients lacked is the most important item in any education for reflective thought."

Aristotle, for example, did not realize that his way of abstracting was only one out of the myriads that are possible, as we know today from the study of Oriental, American Indian, Polynesian, and other languages as well as of the new languages being daily devised by mathematicians and scientists. He regarded his close study of the way in which his language worked not as a study of his language, but as a study of "universal truths." In this respect most people today, including perhaps the majority of "intellectuals," have not progressed beyond Aristotle. Before we can discuss "democracy" or "Teddy bears," they say, we must "define our terms." By defining terms they mean, of course, explaining those words with more words—or, to put it another way, stating in what other cubbyholes those events or experiences which we call "democracy" or "Teddy bears" can be put, according to the rules of our language. That which we call "democracy" can also be put in the cubbyhole marked "forms of government"; that which we call "Teddy bears" can also be put into cubby holes marked "toys."

Like Aristotle, many people today are capable of playing at this verbal game indefinitely in the belief that by so doing they are in some fashion arriving at the "essence" of "Teddy-bearishness" or the "nature" of democracy. In actuality, they are arriving only at a knowledge of what other words or combinations of words can be used, in their dialect, to refer to "Teddy bears" or "democracy." To mistake in this way a description of the rules of one's language for knowledge of things is a glaring instance of failure to distinguish between words and things. Yet, education on the whole makes little attempt to distinguish between knowledge of the rules of consistent discourse and knowledge of the things or processes the words stand for. Students are taught definitions of "democracy," the "electoral system," "executive functions," and so forth. More often than not, they are encouraged to believe that what they have acquired is knowledge of how our government works. Meanwhile, ward heelers who could not give a definition at the point of a gun carry the precincts.

The habit of trusting one's definitions, or, to put it another way, the habit of trusting implicitly the verbal associations, the "clang associations," and the affective disturbances inside one's skin as the result of one's linguistic conditioning (given us constantly by schools, newspapers, radio, preachers, and friends), is one of the most stubborn remnants of primitivism that remain to afflict us. It does not matter if the verbal associations are beautifully systematic, as among the Neo-Aristotelian reformers of modern education, or random, as among the uneducated. Words, and whatever words may suggest, are not the things they stand for, and education that fails to emphasize this fact is more than likely to leave students imprisoned and victimized by their linguistic conditioning, rather than enlightened and liberated by it.

To people so imprisoned, it inevitably appears that if certain individuals have a name in common—say, "criminals" —they must have the "essential attribute" of "criminality" in common, while "noncriminals," of course, do not possess that "attribute." The profound sense that there is something essentially different between people who have been in jail and those who have not is one of the most cherished beliefs both of the respectable rich and the respectable poor. Similarly, as mentioned earlier, Jews are supposed by many to have in common the attribute of "Jewishness," which distinguishes them from non-Jews. Now what is this "Jewishness"? Define it any way you like — take Hitler's definition, or anyone else's— and from that point on, it is not necessary to examine Jews. You know what they are like without even looking, because you have what Aristotle called "knowledge of universals," which "is more precious than sense perceptions and than intuition."

This conviction that the connotations of terms inevitably give insight into the things the terms stand for—this belief that one's categories represent real divisions in nature—is a basic problem, then, in prejudices about race and nationality. No respectable anthropologist today regards as proved a single character difference between races. Even Professor Earnest A. Hooton, who comes as close to "believing in race" as any other anthropologist, agrees that scientific proof of such character differences is still to be discovered. He can only say, as he does in *Man's Poor Relations,* a survey of the known facts about nonhuman primates, that since there are noticeable character differences among different kinds of apes and monkeys, and since different races of men may have descended from different kinds of subhuman primates, different races of men may have inherited some character differences.

Can we learn to take racial and national tags less seriously? Experience teaches some people, of course. Those who, in school, had as playmates children of other racial groups often come out very well trained in this respect. But an amazing number of people who have had the same experiences do not seem to profit from them at all. They often believe, for example, that when they learn that a given person is Jewish, they have found out something quite important about him. Everyone has heard conversations like this: Is Harry Jewish? . . . I don't know. He doesn't look Jewish, does he? . . . Well, in a way he does, and his partner's name certainly sounds Jewish. . . . Oh, I don't know. His wife doesn't look Jewish. . . . No, I guess she doesn't. But you can never tell, can you?

Try to imagine what would happen if a large number of innocents from a far country were brought to the United States and taught how to drive cars. Suppose, moreover, that they were never told what accidents might happen, and therefore were never trained to expect or to try to avoid mishaps. After those motorists were turned loose in traffic for a little while, some lucky ones will have got by without accident, but the majority of those left alive would be chattering with fear, cynical and unbelieving about the advantages claimed for automobile travel, and determined never to trust their lives to an automobile again.

Our traditional educational practices are not unlike such an imagined training for motorists. Children are taught to read and write, and the more "fluently" they talk or write, the higher grades they get. They are trained to respond in specific ways to certain signals: "Christianity" ("a fine thing"), "the Constitution" ("a fine thing"), "Shakespeare" ("a great poet"), "Benedict Arnold" ("a traitor"), and so on. But, especially in the elementary and secondary schools, they are taught very little about how not to respond.

Because Christianity, for example, is highly thought of, an organization practicing the opposite of Christian principles is likely to call itself a "Christian Front"; because the Constitution is a "fine thing," it will occur to an antidemocratic pressure group to call itself a "Committee to Uphold the Constitution"; because Shakespeare was a great poet, it becomes triply important to point out that some of the time he wrote wretched stuff. Every emphasis carries its own dangers, inevitably. However, children are not on the whole given these negative precepts and warnings, often on the ground that they might "destroy faith." But these negative precepts, far from "destroying faith," are the first line of defense of the positive principles a teacher has to offer, in much the same way that knowing when not to step on the gas is the first line of the defense of one's right to go like fury when the circumstances permit.

Traditional education, however, is by no means alone in this matter of teaching people how to respond without telling them how not to respond. Indeed, education is blameless compared to advertising, which spends untold millions to build up connotations, to teach us to put implicit faith in the affective overtones with which "brand names" are invested. "Serutan: if you read it backwards, it spells Natures"; "Mount Vernon: the same square whisky, but in a round bottle"; "How American it is to want something better: Ballantine's"; "In Names We Trust: good, honest products bear good, honest names—Steinway." Advertising, as currently practiced, is almost entirely a matter of pound, pound, pounding into people word-mindedness to the exclusion of fact-mindedness. A number of influences combine, therefore, to produce in us the tendency to rely too much on brand names, political, religious, racial brand names as well as commercial.

Racial and religious classifications have a limited utility. They were useful when they indicated not only race, but geographical origin, language, and culture with a high degree of probability. A Hungarian, at one time, usually came from Hungary, spoke Hungarian, and preferred Hungarian cooking. But times are vastly changed, and in the United States today's Hungarian usually has never been to Hungary, often speaks no Hungarian, and is likely to prefer chicken chow mein to goulash. An American Negro may be anything from black to white, may be a Ph.D. or a chain-gang laborer, may speak a variety of dialects from Harvard to field Gullah, may be capable of anything from murder to winning a Nobel prize. When a man is called a Trobriander, a number of predictions may be made as to his probable habits, knowledge, and tastes. But when a man is called Negro, or Jew, no useful predictions can be made at all, except that a number of people are going to make mistaken predictions. Clearly, then, many racial brand names have ceased to be conveniences.

Since everything in life can be done by Jews as well as non-Jews, by Negroes as well as whites, whether the needs be for janitors, doctors, electricians, pilots, or friends, to be encumbered by brand-name preferences is artificially to restrict oneself to a fraction of the available supply, and as silly as going without coffee simply because your store doesn't have your favorite brand. One inevitably restricts his own freedom whenever he saddles himself with classifications other than useful ones. With racial brand names as with commercial, one has to be able to take 'em or leave 'em alone. I am not trying to say that only semantic reasons account for racial hostility, but I think they explain much of our trouble.

General semantics is, in large part, training in precisely this kind of freedom. Some people are brought up free, and have listened to the radio and gone to school for years without damage to their good sense. Others work themselves out of their imprisonment by empirical tests, as a student of mine once did, who experimentally invited a Jew out for a beer, cultivated his friendship, and found to his amazement that the Jew was a swell guy. (A good engineering student, he handed me a lab report of the experiment.) A similar empirical frame of mind is now being exhibited by some firms who are not only experimentally beginning to hire Negroes, but are trying also to find out the conditions that lead to best race relations. If general semantics merely succeeds in bringing people to try such experiments, it will have done its part.

The trouble with prejudice, however, is that, through endless indoctrination, we are so fully conditioned in our reactions in some situations that, before we are able to say to ourselves "politician$_1$ is not politician$_2$" we have already let go with our trained responses to the word (or "thought") "politician." In matters of race, moreover, set patterns of response are not only taught, but codified in law and custom, with the result that even those who wish to offer Filipino$_3$

a job commensurate with his advanced training and intelligence are prevented from doing so by a society that insists that Filipinos must remain menial servants. Again, the response is dictated in advance of the facts. Our general rule, "A_1 is not A_2," although easy enough to say, is extremely difficult to apply, since it often involves reversing habits of response long established in our nervous systems, and undoing the effects of a lifetime of methodical miseducation.

These are some of the considerations that make students of general semantics as earnest as they are about bringing their principles to the attention of as many people as possible. Teaching people to read and listen, teaching them to write or speak plausibly, glibly, or even beautifully—these are not enough, any more than learning to shift gears and step on the gas is sufficient instruction in driving. Old-fashioned teachers often complain about how little our young people know the meanings of words, and propose to cure this condition by dictionary drill. Whatever merits such a proposal may have, it must not be ignored that, in a sense, young people "know the meaning" of far too many words. They are so full of pat little reactions drilled into them by advertisers, propagandists, teachers, newspapers, parents, and preachers that by the time they get to college half of them have already been rendered uneducable. What practically no one bothers to teach is what words do not mean. Ignorant of the dangers of confusing the verbal patterns inside their heads with the world outside, their education, instead of liberating them, makes them easier marks than they would have been without it.

The proponents of general semantics, therefore, are interested in any kind of education, in school or out and by whatever name, that sharpens peoples' perception of the difference between symbol and thing symbolized, between label and product. Thousands of teachers, despite the unkind things I may have implied about them earlier in this chapter, are daily engaged in this kind of education, as are also a conscientious minority of writers, preachers, movie directors, and publicity men. For example, the monthly magazine *Consumer Reports* is one source of education of this kind.

The liberation of men from race-fetishism is but part of the greater task of releasing them from the last, greatest fetishism, word-fetishism. No semanticist has ever urged anyone to distrust all abstraction. In demanding that people cease reacting to abstract names as if they were realities in themselves, semanticists are merely saying in another way, "Stop acting like suckers."

III

HOW TO LISTEN TO OTHER PEOPLE

THERE are two aspects to communication. One is the matter of output—the speaking and writing, involving problems of rhetoric, composition, logical presentation, coherence, definition of terms, knowledge of the subject and the audience, and so on. Most of the preoccupation with communication is directed toward the improvement of the output, so that we find on every hand courses in composition, in effective speaking, in the arts of plain or fancy talk, and how to write more dynamic sales letters.

But the other aspect of communication, namely, the problem of intake—especially the problem of how to listen well—is relatively a neglected subject. It does not avail the speakers to have spoken well if we as listeners have failed to understand, or if we come away believing them to have said things they didn't say at all. If face-to-face meetings are to result in the exchange of ideas, we need to pay particular heed to our listening habits.

A common difficulty at conferences and meetings is what might be called the "terminological tangle," in which discussion is stalemated by conflicting definitions of key terms. Let me discuss this problem using as examples the vocabulary of art criticism and the discussion of design. What do such terms as "romanticism," "classicism," "baroque," "organic," and "functionalism" *really* mean? Let us put this problem into the kind of context in which it is likely to occur. For example, a speaker may talk about "the romanticism so admirably exemplified by the Robie House by Frank Lloyd Wright." Let us imagine in the audience an individual to whom the Robie House exemplifies many things, but *not* "romanticism." His reaction may well be, "Good God, has he ever *seen* the Robie House?" And he may challenge the speaker to *define* "romanticism"—which is a way of asking, "What do *you* think 'romanticism' really is?" When the speaker has given his definition, it may well prove to the questioner that the speaker indeed doesn't know what he's talking about. But if the questioner counters with an alternative definition, it will prove to the speaker that the questioner doesn't know what *he* is talking about. At this point it will be just as well if the rest of the audience adjourns to the bar, because no further communication is going to take place.

How can this kind of terminological tangle be avoided? I believe it can be avoided if we understand at the outset that there is no ultimately correct and single meaning to words like "romanticism" and "functionalism" and "plastic form" and other items in the vocabulary of art and design criticism. The same is true, of course, of the vocabularies of literary criticism, of politics and social issues, and many other matters of everyday discussion. Within the strictly disciplined contexts of the languages of the sciences, exact or almost exact agreements about terminology can be established. When two physicists talk about "positrons" or when two chemists talk about "diethylene glycol," they can be presumed to have enough of a common background of controlled experience in their fields to have few difficulties about understanding each other. But most of the words of artistic and other general discussion are not restricted to such specialized frames of reference. They are part of the language of everyday life—by which I mean that they are part of the language in which we do not hesitate to speak across occupational lines. The artist, dramatist, and poet do not hesitate to use the vocabularies of their calling in speaking to their audiences; nor would the physician, the lawyer, the accountant, and the clothing merchant hesitate to use these words to one another if they got into a discussion of any of the arts.

In short, the words most commonly used in conference, like the vocabulary of other educated, general discussion, are public property—which is to say that they mean many things to many people. This is a fact neither to be applauded nor regretted; it is simply a fact to be taken into account. They are words, therefore, which either have to be defined anew each time they are seriously used—or, better still, they must be used in such a way, and with sufficient illustrative examples, that their specific meaning in any given discourse emerges from their context.

Hence it is of great importance in a conference to listen to one another's statements and speeches and terminology without unreasonable demands. And the specific unreasonable demand I am thinking of now is the demand that everybody else *should* mean by such words as "romanticism" what I would mean if I were using them. If, therefore, the expression, "the romanticism of the Frank Lloyd Wright Robie House" is one which, at first encounter, makes little sense to us, we should at once be alerted to special attentiveness. The speaker, by classifying the Robie House as "romantic," is making an unfamiliar classification—a sure sign not that he is ill-informed, but that he has a way of classifying his data that is different from our own. And his organization of his data may be one from which we can learn a new and instructive way of looking at the Robie House, or at "romanticism," or at whatever else the speaker may be talking about.

Since a major purpose of conferences is to provide ample opportunity for conversational give-and-take, perhaps it would be wise to consider the adoption, formally or informally, of one basic conversational traffic rule which I have found to be invaluable in ensuring the maximum flow of information and ideas from one person to another, and in avoiding the waste of time resulting from verbal traffic snarls. The rule is easy to lay down, but not always easy to follow: it is that we refrain from agreement or disagreement with a speaker, to refrain from praise or censure of his views, until we are sure what those views are.

Of course, the first way to discover a speaker's views is to listen to him. But few people, other than psychiatrists and women, have had much training in listening. The training of most ververbalized professional intellectuals is in the opposite direction. Living in a competitive culture, most of us are most of the time chiefly concerned with getting our own views across, and we tend to find other people's speeches a tedious interruption of the flow of our own ideas. Hence, it is necessary to emphasize that listening does not mean simply maintaining a polite silence while you are rehearsing in your mind the speech you are going to make the next time you can grab a conversational opening. Nor does listening mean waiting alertly for the flaws in the other fellow's arguments so that later you can mow him down. Listening means trying to see the problem the way the speaker sees it—which means not sympathy, which is *feeling for* him, but empathy, which is *experiencing with* him. Listening requires entering actively and imaginatively into the other fellow's situation and trying to understand a frame of reference different from your own. This is not always an easy task.

But a good listener does not merely remain silent. He asks questions. However, these questions must avoid all implications (whether in tone of voice or in wording) of skepticism or challenge or hostility. They must clearly be motivated by curiosity about the speaker's views. Such questions, which may be called "questions for clarification," usually take the form, "Would you expand on that point about . . . ?" "Would you mind restating that argument about . . . ?" "What exactly is your recommendation again?" Perhaps the most useful kind of question at this stage is something like, "I am going to restate in my words what I think you mean. Then would you mind telling me if I've understood you correctly?"

The late Dr. Irving J. Lee of Northwestern University has suggested another form of questioning which he describes as "the request for information concerning the uniqueness of the particular characteristics of the condition or proposal under consideration." I shall simply call these questions "questions of uniqueness." All too often, we tend to listen to a speaker or his speech in terms of a generalization: "Oh, he's just another of those progressive educators," "Isn't that just like a commercial designer?," "That's the familiar Robsjohn-Gibbings approach," "That's the old Bauhaus pitch," and so on. It is a curious and dangerous fact—dangerous to communication, that is—that once we classify a speech in this way, we stop listening, because, as we say, "We've heard that stuff before." But *this* speech by *this* individual at *this* time and place is a *particular* event, while the "that stuff" with which we are classifying this speech is a *generalization* from the past. Questions of uniqueness are designed to prevent what might be called the functional deafness that we induce in ourselves by reacting to speakers and their speeches in terms of the generalizations we apply to them. Questions of uniqueness take such forms as these: "How large is the firm you work for, and do they make more than one product?" "Exactly what kind of synthetic plastic did you use on that project?" "Are your remarks on abstract expressionism and Jackson Pollock intended to apply equally to the work of De Kooning?"

Something else that needs to be watched is the habit of overgeneralizing from the speaker's remarks. If a speaker is critical of, let us say, the way in which design is taught at a particular school, some persons in the audience seem automatically to assume that the speaker is saying that design shouldn't be taught at all. When I speak on the neglected art of listening, as I have done on many occasions, I am often confronted with the question, "If everybody listened, who would do the talking?" This type of misunderstanding may be called the "pickling-in-brine fallacy," after the senior Oliver Wendell Holmes's famous remark, "Just because I say I like sea bathing, that doesn't mean I want to be pickled in brine." When Korzybski found himself being misunderstood in this way, he used to assert with special forcefulness, "I say what I say; I do not say what I do not say." Questions of uniqueness, properly chosen, prevent not only the questioner but everyone else present from projecting into a speaker's remarks meanings that were not intended.

All too often, the fact that misunderstanding exists is not apparent until deeper misunderstandings have already occurred because of the original one. We have all had the experience of being at meetings or at social gatherings at which Mr. X says something, and Mr. Y believes Mr. X to have said something quite different and argues against what he believes Mr. X to have said. Then Mr. X, not understanding Mr.

Y's objections (which may be legitimate objections to what Mr. X didn't say), defends his original statement with further statements. These further statements, interpreted by Mr. Y in the light of mistaken assumptions, lead to further mistaken assumptions, which in turn induce in Mr. X mistaken assumptions about Mr. Y. In a matter of minutes, the discussion is a dozen miles away from the original topic. Thereafter it can take from twenty minutes to two hours to untangle the mess and restore the discussion to a consideration of Mr. X's original point.

All this is not to say that I expect or wish conversations or conferences to avoid argument. But let us argue about what has been said, and not about what has not been said. And let us discuss not for victory, but for clarification. If we do so, we shall find, I believe, that ultimately agreement and disagreement, approval and disapproval, are not very important after all. The important thing is to come away from a meeting with a fund of information—information about what other people are doing and thinking and why. It is only as we fully understand opinions and attitudes different from our own and the reasons for them that we better understand our own place in the scheme of things. Which is but another way of saying that while the result of communications successfully imparted is self-satisfaction, the result of communications successfully received is self-insight.

IV

THE SELF-CONCEPT

THE Darwinian assertion that "self-preservation is the first law of life" is widely quoted, but I am not at all sure that it is widely believed. Human beings do many things, like working on crossword puzzles, that seems to have very little to do with self-preservation. Or to take further examples: what of the men who work their heads off trying to acquire their tenth million dollars; or the office girls who go without lunch in order to make payments on fur coats that they cannot afford; or the people who risk their lives in the five-hundred-mile races on Memorial Day at Indianapolis, or in expeditions to scale Mount Everest, or in attempts to go over Niagara Falls in a barrel? I myself spend from $150 to $200 a year on equipment and travel to catch about $3.95 worth of fish. All these are characteristic forms of human behavior, but their connection with self-preservation is far from apparent.

Once it is understood that human beings are a symbolic class of life—once it is grasped that all human behavior is conditioned, shaped, and mediated by symbols—then the idea of self-preservation as the first law of life can be modified to include almost all of the complexities of human behavior: the fundamental motive of human behavior is not self-preservation, but the preservation of the symbolic self. If a man symbolizes himself as a certain kind of captain of industry, he must have that tenth, eleventh, or twentieth million dollars. If a woman symbolizes herself as a certain kind of lady of fashion, then that fur coat is much more necessary to her than daily lunch. If a man symbolizes himself as a certain kind of daring sportsman, he must obviously perform feats challenging to his skill and courage.

What I call the symbolic self is much the same as what Carl Rogers calls the "self-concept" and Andras Angyal calls "self-organization." The suggested modification of the Darwinian law of self-preservation can be spelled out more fully thus: The basic purpose of all human activity is the protection, the maintenance, and the enhancement not of the self, but of the self-concept, or symbolic self.

"The self-concept or self-structure," says Rogers, "may be thought of as an organized configuration of perceptions of the self which are admissible to awareness." Human beings are hopelessly addicted to the processes of abstraction, symbolization, and talking to themselves, not only about the world around them, but about themselves. Each of us, therefore, possesses not only a self, but a self-concept.

What Rogers seems to mean when he says that the self-concept is an *organized* configuration of perceptions of the self is that we all try, with whatever degree of success, to make sense to ourselves—to be self-consistent. We like to think that the various aspects of our ideas, beliefs, and goals form some kind of organization—that the various parts of ourselves fit together. We like to feel that we make sense to ourselves, however little sense we may make to our relatives and friends, who may say: "How can he be such a kind man at home and such a tyrant at the office?" "How can he be such a conservative in politics and such a liberal about race relations?" "How can he spend so liberally on books and records and give so little to his church?" Others will see what they regard as inconsistencies and discrepancies in our behavior, but we will not see them. To ourselves we seem consistent. We are "organized."

When Rogers says that the self-concept consists of perceptions of the self *admissible to awareness,* he is acknowledging that some perceptions of the self are not admissible to awareness. We all suppress, to some degree, information that we do not like to face—whether about ourselves or other matters. Therefore, while *unacknowledged* fears or jealousies and repressed memories may be real enough to determine behavior, they are not part of the self-concept, and therefore they are not known to be causes of our actions. The self-concept includes only what we are able to say to ourselves about ourselves.

The self is constantly undergoing change, but the self-concept is slow to change. Just as the map is not the territory, the self-concept is not the self; the map is not all of the territory, and the self-concept likewise never includes all of the self. Furthermore, if the basic purpose of all human activity is the protection, maintenance, and enhancement of the self-concept, we all have a profound urge to become more of what we already are. We want to realize more of our potentialities, and this desire is a basic drive.

Hadley Cantril, Franklin P. Kilpatrick, and others who have worked in the field of perceptual psychology state that the self-concept is the fundamental determinant of our perceptions, and therefore of our behavior. When ten people walk down the same street, they see ten different environments, because each individual has his own background, his own set of values and interests, his own preoccupations—and therefore his own way of extracting meaning from the world around him. The self-concept, in a sense, creates for each of us a unique environment to which to react.

Here in a shop window, let us say, are seventy-five hats, each of them a potential stimulus to the passer-by. A woman walks by—and as she sees one of them she thinks, "That's a hat I must have!" and, busy as she is, she must run in to buy it before she can go on. Why is it that that one item in a complex environment almost jumps out to catch her attention? The reason is that since the basic purpose of the organism is to enhance the self-concept, if there is something in the environment that would be enhancing to that self-concept, the perceptual processes reach out, as it were, to react to it. As John Dewey said, "A stimulus becomes a stimulus by virtue of what the organism was already preoccupied with." That hat will look very well on the lady's self-concept—however it may look on her.

The self-concept, of course, is not always an accurate map of the territory of the self. How do unrealistic elements get into the self-concept? Let us say that a child develops—as children do—a fear of dogs. Let us further imagine that the child has a father who says, "Anybody who is afraid of dogs is a sissy, and no sissy is a boy of mine." The child is confronted with a dilemma. He must either acknowledge his fear of dogs and be rejected by his father, or overcome or conceal his fear to retain his father's love. If this fear cannot be immediately overcome, as such fears frequently cannot, he says both to himself and his father, "I am not afraid of dogs. See, Dad, I'm not afraid of dogs!" until he believes it himself. The fear is thus driven underground, into the unconscious.

Suppose a man says, "I am the best salesman in my company," and suppose further that the statement is true. But time passes. Two new men are hired who begin to turn in better records. Imagine also a well-brought-up young woman, firmly brought up to believe that a lady has no sexual feelings, who begins, in late adolescence, to experience them. Threats to the self-concept may come, as in the case of the salesman, from the outside world, as in the case of the young lady, from within.

Life presents many occasions on which we must mobilize ourselves against threatening circumstances. Here, let us say, is another little boy, who has never been in a big lake before. Shall he go into the water? He is attracted by the idea because there are other children in there splashing around and enjoying themselves. But the encounter with this new experience is also frightening. The father at this point may offer to take the child's hand or to carry him in, thus reducing the threat and enabling the child to acquire this new experience. Some fathers are not so tactful: they may throw the child in with, "There's nothing to be afraid of, boy; it's only eighteen inches deep." That there is nothing to be afraid of *for the father* doesn't mean a thing *to the child* at the moment. It is at times like this that the child, like all of us, needs psychological support, so that he will gain the courage to confront the threat. Suppose, however, that the threat is so great that the boy never does muster up enough courage to go into the water. Then mechanisms of rationalization go into effect.

Rationalization is the defense by means of which the self-concept is shielded against the need for reorganization: "I am the best salesman in the company, no matter what the records show. It's just that the company is now giving me all the worst territory." "I am a lady; I don't feel any sexual impulses whatsoever." "I didn't want to go in the water anyway. Besides, mother says there are germs in there." It is thus that rigidity of personality is developed. The self-concept becomes rigidified in an attempt to keep out disturbing perceptions, whether from the outside world or from within.

When the self-concept is thus rigidified, it may remain unchanged for a while. Trouble arises from the fact that the *self* will not stay put. The self slips away from the self-concept; the individual's ideas about himself become less and less real as time goes on. In other words, it may originally have been true that the man was the best salesman in the company, but as time goes on and the facts of life change, it will require more and more self-delusion on his part to maintain his self-concept. In Willie Loman of his *Death of a Salesman*, Arthur Miller gives a terrifyingly accurate account of self-delusion in the defense of a no longer realistic self-concept.

Conflict is essential to growth. Conflict that cannot be resolved, however, results in more or less serious emotional disturbance. The longer the conflict remains unresolved, the more serious does the emotional disturbances become, and the more does the self-concept depart from the reality of the self. As Korzybski says, prediction and control are possible only when maps correspond to the territories they represent. If the self-concept remains unchanging while the self continues to change, the disparity between map and territory increases, so that there is progressive decrease in one's ability to predict and control his own behavior.

Let us put another ending to the story of the salesman. Let us suppose that in the light of changing circumstances he says, "Those two new men are really pretty good. Now we have three first-rate salesmen in our company!" The immediate implication of such a reorganized view of himself is, "I am no longer a lone wolf; I am a member of a team." Once the individual reorganizes his self-concept to that degree, he becomes able to modify his behavior correspondingly. Thus he may discover capacities for co-operation and teamwork in himself that he had formerly never had occasion to explore. It is through such reorganizations of the self-concept that the individual discovers more and more about himself—and becomes more mature—as time goes on.

"Learning," as Prescott Lecky says, "begins with a problem which produces or threatens to produce an emergency state." The process of learning, which is also the process of growth, is "essentially a means of resolving conflicts. . . . A conflict must always be present before learning can occur. . . . Conflict then is a necessary accompaniment of personality development, and the progressive assimilation of disturbing stimuli the only practical means by which a stable organization can be attained." Without conflict, "neither neurosis nor learning results." One implication of this idea is that providing security for children is a process that can easily be carried too far. A security that is designed to shield children from all problems may well have the effect of shielding them from all occasions for learning, because it is only through problems and conflicts that the learning process can take place.

Where does the self-concept come from? Certainly the formation of the self-concept must begin in the cradle. The baby touches his toes and his blanket and his rattle and learns which of these is part of himself—what is "me" and what is "not me." Long before the baby is able to walk, he receives many subverbal messages that must also help to form his self-concept. If he understands, from the way in which he is fed and held, that he is loved and cherished, he grows up feeling, "I am loved; someone will always love me." Alternatively, the child may grow up feeling rejected. Such messages are communicated to the baby by touch, by gesture, and by tone of voice long before he is able to understand words.

Later the parents talk to the child, and over the course of years they build up, consciously or unconsciously—but mostly unconsciously—through behavior and words, all sorts of ideas by means of which the child structures his self-concept. The cultural role of the girl, as opposed to that of the boy, is sharply differentiated quite early. At a tender age the little girl is told, "Now you mustn't do that, Marie, because you are a little girl, and girls don't do that"—whatever "that" may be. Many such cultural imperatives are established—and internalized by the little boy or girl.

Many items in the self-concept are acquired by the child through overhearing the remarks of the parents, because some parents have the habit of talking about their children in their presence but as if they were not there: "I don't know what to do about Jimmy; he's so hopelessly shy. And isn't it a shame about Florence's hair!" And there is little Florence sitting on the floor developing feelings of inferiority and inadequacy! Then, of course, there are many direct statements: "Why aren't *you* at the head of your class?" "Why don't you practice your piano? Elaine practices two hours a day." Or the other kind of statement: "You are the most important thing in all the world!" All these statements, both verbal and nonverbal, help to create the self-concept.

The self-concept also results from personal evaluations, personal experiences. At a certain age, we begin to make comparisons of ourselves with others: "I can run faster than Ricky"; "Michael is stronger than I am"; "I am afraid of dogs, but I love cats." This process of noting one's own reactions to things goes on, of course, for the rest of life: "I find I like bridge"; "It's exciting to be a security salesman"; "I love going to the Museum of Modern Art"; "I can't stand string quartets." From all these experiences and evaluations, we accumulate the materials of our self-concepts and correct and modify them as time goes on. Insofar as these statements about the self are based on experience and behavior patterns and reactions that we have observed in ourselves without distortion or self-deception, we have healthy and realistic self-concepts.

Included in the self-concept should be a knowledge of how

much more there is to know about oneself. There is an old joke about a man who was asked if he could play a violin and answered, "I don't know. I've never tried." This is psychologically a very wise reply. Those who have never tried to play a violin really do not know whether they can or not. Those who say too early in life and too firmly, "No, I'm not at all musical," shut themselves off prematurely from whole areas of life that might have proved rewarding. In each of us there are unknown possibilities, undiscovered potentialities—and one big advantage of having an open self-concept rather than a rigid one is that we shall continue to expose ourselves to new experiences and therefore we shall continue to discover more and more about ourselves as we grow older.

Emotional identification also plays an important role in the formation of the self-concept. (I now use the word "identification" in a sense different from that intended in Chapter I.) The earliest form of this identification is, "I want to grow up and be like my daddy (or mother)." One of the functions of adults is to provide the young with models upon which the next generation may pattern itself. Early in life children find models outside the family for imitation and emulation: older children in the neighborhood; characters in movies or comic books or other fiction; athletic heroes; sometimes much admired and loved teachers. Many roles are chosen, which children try out for varying lengths of time: The Lone Ranger, Cheyenne, Superman, Robin Hood, Mickey Mantle, D'Artagnan in *The Three Musketeers,* Martin Arrowsmith, James Dean, or Marlon Brando. (At the age of twenty-two, I was role-playing T. S. Eliot, when I wasn't being Oscar Wilde.) With the enactment of each role, the boy learns a little more about about his own feelings, his abilities, his likes and dislikes, his limitations and his possibilities. This long period of role-playing in the life of every boy and girl is a necessary part of the process of defining the self-concept.

Parenthetically, I have often wondered why there are so many exciting masculine roles to emulate described in literature and the popular arts, and relatively so few challenging feminine roles. The girls' and women's magazines offer models of beauty, charm, popularity, and domesticity—all desirable enough goals no doubt, but certainly lacking in the challenge of personal exploit. Is it that girls don't need models to emulate as much as boys do, because girls have at home a model in their mothers? Or is there in the United States a vast social conspiracy against women—a conspiracy to make the girl feel guilty or unfeminine if she wants to distinguish herself, like Joan of Arc, Florence Nightingale, Madame Curie, or Eleanor Roosevelt, through personal achievement? I incline to the latter view, and I am sure that those American women who wanted to get into space before Valentina Tereshkova but were prevented from doing so by the policies of the National Aeronautics and Space Administration will agree with me.

What we admire, we emulate. For this reason, Dr. Frederic Wertham is probably right when he argues in *Seduction of the Innocent* (1954) that crime and horror comic books are among the causes of juvenile crimes of violence. Advertising, too, provides models for us to live up to—models of fashion and elegance and "gracious living." Oscar Wilde once remarked that "Life is the imitation of art." I do not know if Wilde was being serious or merely toying, as he was wont to do, with paradox when he said this. But I am willing to take the remark seriously. Imaginative representations, whether in the form of books, plays, movies, advertising, or comic books, all help to shape our dreams, our dramatizations of ourselves, our self-concepts, and therefore our behavior.

To return, then, to the problems of communication: if it is true that everybody is trying to protect and enhance his self-concept, then your messages get through not only because you have presented them eloquently or logically, but more pertinently because of the meanings they have to the listener in the light of his interests and his self-concept. If the content of your message is seen by your listener as enhancing to his self-concept, it will be received and welcomed. If, however, the ideas you are trying to present are seen by the listener as threatening, all he will do is rigidify his defenses against you. The harder you talk, the more skillfully you talk, the more plausible you become, the more suspicious and defensive he becomes. No man or woman can easily be persuaded to do something, to accept something, which violates or threatens his self-concept. Nor can a child. Here is Prescott Lecky on the subject of boys being taught to read; the passage is from his *Self-Consistency: A Theory of Personality* (1945):

"The boy from six to eight years old, just beginning to learn to read, is mainly concerned with maintaining the conception of himself as manly. He likes to play cowboy, G-man, and Indian. He tries not to cry when he gets a bump. Yet this boy, when the reading lesson begins, must stand up before his companions and read that 'the little red hen says "Cluck! Cluck! Cluck!"'—or something equally inconsistent with his standards of how he should behave. To be obliged to read such material aloud, especially in the presence of others, is not consistent with his view of masculine values. . . . When books on railroads and airplanes are provided, they serve to support these values and are assimilated eagerly."

Lecky finds the self-concept theory useful, too, in explaining the problem student who does well in everything except spelling:

"This deficiency is not due to a lack of ability, but rather to an active resistance which prevents him learning how to spell in spite of extra instruction. The resistance arises from the fact that at some time in the past the suggestion that he is a poor speller was accepted and incorporated into his definition of himself. . . . His difficulty is thus explained as a special instance of the general principle that a person can only be true to himself. If he defined himself as a poor speller, the misspelling of a certain proportion of the words which he uses becomes for him a moral issue. He misspells words for the same reason that he refuses to be a thief."

(I hope I may be forgiven for giving so many examples from the education of the young. I do so partly because I am a teacher—and a teacher of teachers—but mainly because children provide easily understood and easily remembered paradigms of problems of communication at all levels. Even international problems, someone once said, are problems of child psychology.)

Still another facet of the self-concept is one's self-definition as a member of a group: "I am a Boy Scout," "I am a member of Rotary," "I am a United States Marine." Such group self-concepts are also an important determinant of behavior. One of my students, a fourth-grade teacher, reports meeting at one time an almost solid wall of resistance when she tried to teach her class fractions. They simply turned a deaf ear to the subject, although they were doing well enough in all their other arithmetic. By keeping a few of her pupils after school to chat with them, she learned that her class defined itself as the class to whom no one could teach fractions! Their previous teacher had failed, a substitute teacher had failed, and even the curriculum co-ordinator from the county superintendent's office had failed to teach them fractions. They naturally felt that if they learned fractions, they would lose their chief claim to fame. When the teacher learned of this group self-concept, she was able to handle the problem by giving them the chance to change it from "nobody can teach us fractions" to "we can learn fractions better than anybody." The class was far from being stupid; it was simply a class with a strong group morale. That morale could stand in the way of the teacher's purposes, or, understood by the teacher, it could be used to achieve her purposes. The important thing about this incident was that the teacher listened to her pupils long enough to find out what the problem was.

A plan to reorganize the routines of an office in the interests of greater efficiency may arouse tremendous opposition among the employees. To the employer, their resistance to the new idea may seem to be plain foolishness. But how can the employer know, unless he listens to his employees carefully, what individual self-concepts or group loyalties are being threatened by his reorganization plan?

All God's children have self-concepts. All God's children try to protect, maintain, and enhance their self-concepts within the environment as they see it, which is not the same as the environment as you see it. The other fellow has goals which make sense to him, which may not be your goals. If you try to force or to impose your perceptions and goals on the other fellow, he may feel threatened. If he feels threatened, he will resist your communications. This resistance is not so much proof of his cussedness as it is evidence that, like yourself, he sees what he sees, he understands what he understands, and he is not likely to change his perceptions just because someone tells him to.

Here, let us say, is a bowl with goldfish in it. The bowl is inadequate; the water is stale and there is not enough room for all the goldfish. Here, too, is a brand-new aquarium with fresh running water which you have just brought home. For their own good, you would like to transfer the fish from the bowl to the aquarium. But when you try to catch them in your hand net, they see the net as threatening and energetically resist capture. So you have to go after them forcibly and dump them in the new aquarium whether they like it or not. When goldfish resist what is good for them, we do not get impatient with them for their stupidity, because we accept the fact that we cannot reason with them.

When human beings refuse to do something that we think is good for them, we sometimes get impatient with them; sometimes we treat them as if they were goldfish and force our wishes upon them—or try to. But human beings are not gold-fish, and when they resist our wishes, they can resist effectively. If they resist, what can we do? We have to find out first of all the *meaning* of what we have asked of them—not the meaning to ourselves, which we know already, but the meaning to them. What is the meaning of a lesson in fractions from the pupils' point of view? What is the meaning of the office reorganization from the employees' point of view? When you know what the meaning of an idea is to the other fellow and how it differs from the meanings you find in it yourself, you know what the semantic barrier is that stands between you and him.

When communication is blocked, says Carl Rogers, the thing to do is to suspend the pursuit of your own goals and listen to the other fellow—and find out how the world looks to him. If we really want to facilitate the communicative process, he says, we must learn to listen "nonevaluatively," which means listening without passing judgments, favorable or unfavorable, on what the other fellow is saying. If we can really listen, with a desire to understand and with genuine intellectual curiosity as to how the other fellow arrives at conclusions so different from our own, we automatically relax his defenses, because he no longer finds us threatening. Because he does not find us threatening, he reduces the threatening quality of his own behavior, so that we find our own defenses relaxing too. A benign cycle of mutual relaxation of tensions can set in, once this interaction is started.

In our complex and interrelated world, in which the need to understand and to be understood is greater than it has ever been, the cry arises on every hand: "How can we communicate better?" "How can we avoid being misunderstood?" "How can we get our message across?" "How can we improve our image?"

perhaps the wrong questions are being asked. Perhaps the right questions are: "How can we become better listeners?" "How can we better understand the views of others?"

Perhaps the way to overcome the semantic barrier is not to redouble our efforts to "pierce the Iron Curtain" that divides us from those with whom we strongly disagree. Perhaps the best thing we can do is to attempt energetically and imaginatively to enter the other fellow's frame of reference so that we understand what he is talking about. When communications are established from him to us, a channel is established which works equally well for communications from us to him. A constant awareness of the two-way nature of the communicative process is essential to the improvement of human relations, whether between parent and child, teacher and student, employer and employee, or nation and nation.

V

THE FULLY FUNCTIONING

PERSONALITY

THERE are two views of security, namely, the static and the dynamic. The static concept of security may be pictured by thinking of the oyster inside its shell, the frightened person behind his neurotic defenses, or prewar France behind the Maginot Line. The main idea in the static concept of security is to build up enough protective walls and to sit still inside them. The search for security for many people still is the task of building and maintaining walls around oneself.

The dynamic concept of security can be pictured by thinking of a skillful and self-confident driver speeding home in the traffic stream along the highway. He knows that the highway is dangerous; he knows that he may encounter drunken drivers or cars with faulty brakes, and he knows that a slight error in judgment at sixty miles an hour may result in his not getting home at all. Nevertheless, he is not insecure, he is not frightened; in fact, this daily confrontation of danger doesn't worry him at all, because his security in this dynamic and dangerous situation depends not on walls to protect him from danger, but on internal resources—skill, knowledge, experience, flexibility—with which he knows he can cope with danger.

And in this choice of examples I think I have already indicated that the static concept of security is an illusory one, except perhaps for oysters—and who wants to be an oyster?

Assuming, however, that the search for security has been successful, and that there has been developed a person who is genuinely free of neurotic anxieties, and therefore free of needless defensive reactions, what would he (or she) look like? What sort of a person would a genuinely sane individual be? What would he be like to have around, to talk with as a friend, to work with as a colleague? That is, how does he distinguish himself from people like us?

I am interested in this topic because there is plenty of literature on neurotics and psychotics, telling us how we got to be the messes we are: through being bottle-fed or through not being bottle-fed, through being toilet-trained too severely, through living in an overcompetitive culture, through having sexual inhibitions or through having not enough of them, through having had the wrong parents, through having been subjected to the wrong methods of education, and so on. We have thousands of descriptions of emotional disturbance and its causes. But we have few descriptions of emotional health. And so, as I say, what does a sane person look like?

One of the bases of my inquiry is Korzybski's claim that he gave the first clear, definite, functional definition of sanity. The sane individual, he said, does not confuse levels of abstraction; he does not treat the map as if it were the territory; he does not copy animals in their reactions, and therefore is not a *dog*matist or a *cat*egorist (the pun is Korzybski's, not mine) ; he does not treat as identical all things that have the same name; he does not exhibit two-valued orientations in which absolute good is pitted against absolute evil; he does not confuse reports with inferences, inferences with judgmental statements; he is cautious about applying generalizations to particulars, and so on.

You will note that this description of the sane individual is a negative description, because it says so many things that he does not do. Of course, there are positive elements in Korzybski's description of sanity, too. They are to the effect that the sane individual is extensionally oriented (that is, he is fact-minded rather than word-minded), he is conscious of his abstracting process and of his projecting processes, he is relaxed rather than rigid or defensive, and he is co-operative and mature in his orientations.

I do not wish to argue with Korzybski's concept of sanity, which I believe is as good as any you can find. Nevertheless, his account of sanity is at a fairly high level of abstraction. He said, for example, that if our evaluative processes were not crippled by built-in misevaluations, we would all function so well that we could be regarded as geniuses. Some people have laughed at Korzybski because they thought that he made a vast overstatement when he said this, but I don't think there is anything to laugh at here. We all know people, including people who are very dear to us among our friends and relatives, who we feel would be enormously creative if they only got the bugs out of their systems. Often we feel that way about ourselves. Hence, to cease being crippled by unsound evaluative habits does not seem to me an unrealizable goal. Maybe we could all be geniuses, or at least a little less removed from the genius class, if we knew how to overcome our misevaluations. But again let me call attention to the fact that the main emphasis of Korzybski's description of sanity is a negative one, that is, that we must stop doing the things we do now that prevent us from functioning better. And so we do not get a picture from Korzybski of the semantically liberated or the sane individual.

Professor A. H. Maslow of Brandeis University has done a study of what he calls the "self-actualizing person" in his book *Motivation and Personality*. Also, Dr. Carl Rogers of the University of Chicago, in his book *On Becoming a Person,* has been trying to isolate the characteristics of what he calls the "fully functioning person" or the "creative person." From their work and that of others in the same general direction, we get a picture of what modern psychologists—specifically those psychologists whose position is most closely allied to that of general semantics—regard as the psychologically healthy person, that is, the person whose search for security has been successful.

So I shall discuss the "genuinely sane person" or, to use Rogers's term, the "fully functioning person." What does he look like? Who is this character? Rogers's theories are based upon an extrapolation from observations abstracted from successful cases of therapy that he has seen, and the materials for his pictures of the "sane person" are the experiences and clinical records of a psychotherapist. Maslow approaches his idea of the "sane person," whom he calls the "self-actualizing personality," from a different source. He defines the "self-actualizing person" as one who makes "full use and exploitation of his talents, capacities, and potentialities." These people, he says, "seem to be fulfilling themselves and to be doing the best that they are capable of doing. They are people who have developed or are developing to the full stature of which they are capable."

In order to isolate the characteristics of the "self-actualizing personality," Maslow started with a rough definition and applied it to those of his friends, acquaintances, and students who seemed to fill the bill. He also studied a number of historical characters and living personalities, about sixty or seventy people altogether, who seemed to meet the requirements. He does not always give the names of the persons he has studied. Some of them were famous, some obscure. Some he thought to be self-actualizing turned out, on closer examination, not to be as healthy as they looked at first. After much careful screening, he narrowed down his list to some forty people whom he found to be self-actualizing to a large degree.

Hence I shall lump together Rogers's "fully functioning person" with Maslow's "self-actualizing personality" and call this combined abstraction the "genuinely sane individual."

The most impressive fact, as described by both Rogers and Maslow, is that these sane people are not, in the ordinary sense of the term, "well-adjusted." The unreflective layman and many schoolteachers and administrators, even some psychiatrists, seem to believe that adjustment to a society, in the sense of complete conformity with the goals, internal and external, of that society, is the goal of mental health. Such a view of adjustment would mean that in Rome you would not only do as the Romans do, but think and feel as the Romans do; that in a money-mad society you, too, would be money-mad; that in a Nazi society you would be a good Nazi. The fully functioning personality is not, in that sense, fully adjusted. His relation to the society around him may be described somewhat as follows: He is *in* and *of* society of which he is a member, but he is not a prisoner of that society.

On the other hand, the fully functioning personality is not an outright rebel against the social norms of a society either, given a halfway tolerable society to live in. Maslow writes as follows of his case studies of self-actualizing personalities:

"Their behavior is marked by simplicity and naturalness, and by lack of artificiality and straining for effort. This does not necessarily mean consistently unconventional behavior.

Actually the 'self-actualizing personality' is not extremely un-conventional. His unconventionality is not superficial but essential and internal. It is his impulse, thought, and conscious-ness that are unconventional, spontaneous and natural. Apparently recognizing that the world of people in which he lives could not understand or accept this, and since he has no wish to hurt people or to fight them over trivialities, he will go through the ordinary trivial conventions with a good-humored shrug and with the best possible grace. . . . But the fact that this 'conventionality' is a cloak which rests very lightly on his shoulders and is easily cast aside can be seen from the fact that the self-actualizing person practically never allows convention to hamper him or inhibit him from doing anything that he considers very important and basic."

Rogers states just about the same thing when he says, "The fully functioning personality is not necessarily 'ad-justed' to his culture, he is not a conformist. But at any time and in any culture he would live constructively, in as much harmony with the culture as a balanced satisfaction of his internal needs demanded." In other words, he can take his culture or he can leave it alone, as dictated by his deepest inner needs.

This, too, can be restated in the language of general seman-tics. A fundamental idea of general semantics is that human beings are a symbolic class of life, from which insight follow our generalizations about the relationships between symbols and what they stand for. Because we are a symbolic class of life, much of our behavior, many of our needs, are symbolic in addition to being functional.

Let me illustrate this in a humble way. When we are hun-gry, of course we must eat, but we often eat at more expen-sive restaurants than we can afford because we hope to sym-bolize by this choice of restaurant our high social status, and we want to avoid the distasteful low-status symbolism of the modest restaurant where the food is better and the prices are lower. To those whose symbol-systems are fixated and who have no self-insight, eating at the most expensive restaurant in town *is* success, while eating anywhere else *is* social disgrace. For the symbol-fixated people this kind of identity equation holds for all other social symbols in the way of conspicuous consumption, social rituals, and social behavior. These are the people whose self-respect is *absolutely* dependent on the kind of clothes they wear, the kind of car they drive, the kind of society they are seen with. For these people clothes or cars or country-club membership or social ritual are not symbols, but ultimate realities.

To know the difference between a symbol and that which is symbolized—the difference between map and territory—is a central idea in semantics. Of course others before Korzybski had made this observation, but Korzybski was alone in making this a central premise of his thinking. Once you have internalized the idea that the symbol is not that which is symbolized, then you come to realize that never to have been invited to join the country club does not mean that your life has been lived in vain, and, per contra, it also means that you are able to dine at the country club, when you have to, without acting as if it was going to kill you.

In general semantics terms, the optimum relations of an individual to his culture can be stated as follows: since the map is not the territory, since the symbol is not that which is symbolized, the semantically well-orientated person is primarily concerned with the territory and not with the map, with the social reality rather than the social façade.

A second fact about the sane person is that, to an unusual degree, his own feelings and emotions, his own resentments and tensions, his attractions and his dislikes, are, in Rogers's terms, "accessible to awareness." We all have some kind of self-concept or self-image. Thus, we may think of ourselves as efficient or inefficient, hard-boiled or kindhearted, lovable or unlovable, artistic or practical, and so on. But also we all have impulses and feelings that do not fit our self-concepts, in that the man who thinks of himself as hard-boiled and tough may feel a twinge of humane sentiment that he would not know what to do with, or the person who thinks of himself as extremely gentle may suddenly find in himself a sadistic impulse. The self-defined highbrow may feel a lowbrow urge to go to a prize fight, while the husband who has been openly scornful of his wife's interest in modern art may unexpectedly find himself warming up to a painting by Miró. What so-called "normal" people do with these wellings of unexpected feeling that arise inside of them is to suppress them, to deny them to awareness, since to admit them to awareness would mean the reorganization of their picture of themselves.

The way in which a genuinely psychologically healthy person differs from so-called "normal" people in this respect is in the fact that he is aware of his own feelings, he does not try to suppress them, he often acts upon them, and, even if he does not act upon them, he is able to admit them to awareness. Let me quote Rogers's description of this characteristic:

"This person would be open to his own experience. . . . In a person who is open to his experience . . . every stimulus, whether originating in the organism or in his environment, would be freely relayed through the nervous system without being distorted by defensive mechanisms."

Rogers talks about one of his patients: "Formerly he could not freely feel pain or illness, because being ill meant for him being unacceptable. Neither could he feel tenderness and love for his child, because such feelings meant being weak, and he had to maintain his façade of being strong. After therapy he can be genuinely open to the experiences of his organism—he can be tired when he is tired, he can feel pain when his organism is in pain, he can freely experience the love he feels for his daughter, and he can also feel and express the annoyance for her when he feels annoyed . . . he can fully live the experiences of his total organism, rather than shutting them out of his awareness. I have used this concept of availability to awareness to try to make clear what I mean by openness to one's own experience. This might be misunderstood. I do not mean that this individual would be self-consciously aware of all that was going on in himself, like the centipede that became aware of all his legs. On the contrary, he would be free to live a feeling subjectively, as well as be aware of it. He might experience love, or pain, or fear. Or he might abstract himself from this subjectivity and realize in awareness, 'I am in pain,' 'I am afraid,' 'I do love.' But the crucial point is that there are no barriers inside himself, no inhibitions which would prevent the full experiencing of his own emotions."

Maslow also is interested in this subject, and it is curious how he and Rogers converge from different theoretical sources. Maslow says of the self-actualizing personality, "Their ease of penetration to reality, their closer approach to an animal-like or child-like acceptance and spontaneity imply a superior awareness of their own impulses, their own desires, opinions, and subjective reactions in general."

These characteristics can be translated into the language of general semantics. The first fundamental postulate of general semantics, as already indicated, is that the map is not the territory, and the second postulate is that the map is never *all* of a territory. Now, if we regard the self-concept as the map of the self, we can, if we confuse the map with the territory, feel that the self-concept *is* the self, which it is not. In other words, if my self-concept defines me as a gentle, kind-hearted person, then *by definition* I don't *ever* have any cruel or sadistic impulses. If sadistic impulses occur, they have to be denied to awareness. In other words, if my self-definition as gentle and kindhearted is rigid enough, I cannot permit myself to be aware of my nonkindhearted impulses, rare as they may be. Therefore, in one respect at least, I shall be like the famous man who shouted, "You know goddam well I never lose my temper!"

Supposing, on the other hand, I were a good general semanticist, aware through internalization of the principle that the map is not all the territory, that the self-concept is not all of the self. In such a case I should, even if I defined myself as "gentle and tenderhearted," realize that this definition does not say all about myself, and therefore I should be compelled to state, "So far as I know, and in the situations in which I have found myself, I have been, up to now, on the whole, gentle and tenderhearted. But since I have not been in all possible situations, nor experienced all possible experiences, and since few of us are completely honest with ourselves, there no doubt exist within me feelings I have not recognized in myself, as well as potentialities for emotions that I have not yet had occasion to feel." With such an attitude toward our own self-definitions, we should indeed be, in Rogers's terminology, "open to our own experience."

In short, the serious student of general semantics, as of any other psychological discipline, extending his scientific principles to every concept, including his own concept of himself, would know that every map, including the map of the self, must shade off at the edges into a terra incognita. Therefore he expects the unexpected within the area of his own thoughts and feelings, and he is not compelled to deny these feelings to awareness.

Socrates said, "Know thyself." But he also said, "Whatever authority I may have, rests solely upon my knowing how little I know." And what Socrates said about knowledge in general applies with special cogency to self-knowledge. The individual who says, "I know myself," does not know himself.

It is the individual who knows how little he knows about himself who stands a reasonable chance of finding out something about himself before he dies.

Another thing about the genuinely sane person that is emphasized, although in different ways, by Rogers and Maslow is that since the map is not the territory, and since, therefore, knowledge about an event is never the event itself, those who take this fact for granted are not uncomfortable about the fact that they don't know the answers. Maslow says, "Our healthy subjects are uniformly unthreatened and unfrightened by the unknown, being therein quite different from average men. They accept the unknown, they are comfortable with it, and, often are even attracted by it. To use Frenkel-Brunswick's phrase, 'they can tolerate the ambiguous.' . . . Since, for healthy people, the unknown is not frightening, they do not have to spend any time laying the ghost, whistling past the cemetery, or otherwise protecting themselves against danger. They do not neglect the unknown, or deny it, or run away from it, or try to make believe it really is known, nor do they organize, dichotomize, or rubricize it prematurely. They do not cling to the familiar, nor is their quest for truth a catastrophic need for certainty, for safety, for definiteness, and order." And this next sentence by Maslow is one that I find especially attractive: "The fully-functioning personality can be, when the objective situation calls for it, comfortably disorderly, anarchic, vague, doubtful, uncertain, indefinite, approximate, inexact, or inaccurate."

There is another fundamental principle of general semantics with which many of you are perfectly familiar, namely, that of indexing and dating, as we call it in our lingo. The idea is, of course, that no two individual things or persons or events are ever identical, and that everything in the world is in process, with changes occurring constantly. We have that rule in the form A_1 is not A_2; most of our errors of evaluation arise from identification reactions, in which we ignore the differences between individuals of the same class name, and in which we ignore the changes that occur over time.

Another name for the same principle in general semantics literature is extensionality, as opposed to intensionality. The extensional individual responds to similarities *and differences;* whereas the intensional individual tends to ignore differences among things that have the same name. This principle of intensional orientation is illustrated by the belief "A woman driver is, after all, a woman driver." The extensional individual is highly aware of things, people, and events at subverbal levels, where everything is in process and everything is in change.

Maslow and Rogers describe the fully functioning personality as extensional, although they do not use the term. In Rogers's paper "Towards a Theory of Creativity," this concept of openness to experience is elaborated. He says, "The creative person, instead of perceiving in predetermined categories ('trees are green,' 'college education is a good thing,' 'modern art is silly') is aware of this existential moment as it *is,* and therefore he is alive to many experiences which fall outside the usual categories (in *this* light this tree is purple; *this* college education is damaging; *this* modern sculpture has a powerful effect on me).

"The creative person is in this way open to his own experiences. It means a lack of rigidity and the permeability of boundaries in concepts, beliefs, perceptions and hypotheses. It means a tolerance of ambiguity where ambiguity exists. It means the ability to receive much conflicting information without forcing closure on the situation."

Maslow has another way of saying this: "Self-actualized people have a wonderful capacity to appreciate again and again, freshly and naively the basic goods of life, with awe, pleasure, wonder, and even ecstasy, however stale these experiences may be for other people. Thus, for such people, every sunset is as beautiful as the first one, any flower can be breathtakingly lovely even after he has seen a million flowers. And the thousandth baby he sees is just as miracu-lous a product as the first one he saw." And this is simply an-other way of stating the indexing principle. Thus, $sunset_1$ is not $sunset_2$; $flower_{1,000,000}$ is not $flower_{1,000,001}$; $baby_{1000}$ is not $baby_{1001}$. Therefore experience continues to be fresh for the creative person.

Maslow describes this extensionality of self-actualizing people in social relationships in the following terms: "They can be and are friendly with anyone of suitable character re-gardless of class, education, political belief, race or color. As a matter of fact it seems as if they are not even aware of the differences which often mean so much to other people." In other words, the self-actualizing person *experiences at lower levels of abstraction* than the rest of us; he reacts to the spe-cific $Smith_1$, $Smith_2$, and therefore he concerns himself very little with high-order abstractions such as "He is a Catholic," "He is a Republican," "He is a Negro."

Maslow also says, "The first and most obvious level of acceptance to be found in the self-actualizing personality is at the so-called animal level. These self-actualizing people tend to be good and lusty animals, hearty in their appetites and enjoying themselves mightily without regret or shame or apology. They seem to have a uniformly good appetite for food, they seem to sleep well, they seem to enjoy their sexual lives without unnecessary inhibition, and so on for all the rel-atively physiological impulses. They are able to 'accept' themselves not only at these lower levels, but at all levels as well, e.g., love, safety, belongingness, honor, self-respect. All these are accepted without question as worth while simply because they are part of human nature, and because these people are inclined to accept the work of nature rather than argue with nature for not having constructed things to a different plan. This interesting point shows itself in self-actualizing people by the lack of disgusts and aversions seen in average people and especially in neurotics, e.g., food annoyances, disgust with body products, body odors, and body functions." As Maslow explains further: "One does not complain about water because it is wet, nor about rocks because they are hard. . . . As the child looks out upon the world with wide, uncritical and innocent eyes, simply noting and observing what is the case, without either arguing the matter or demanding that it be otherwise, so does the self-actualizing person look upon human nature both in himself and others.

Another curious fact, which I find deeply meaningful and which Maslow points out, arises from this childlike quality of perception and feeling in the self-actualized person which makes for a structure of ends and means different from those of other people. For most people, almost everything they do is a means to an end. So far as people who are regarded as normal in the rat race of American life are concerned, ends are often almost impossible to discover: they work in order to eat, they eat in order to work; or they play golf in order to keep fit, and they keep fit in order to work better, and they work better in order to be able to afford their golf-club fees. Maslow says that people even rationalize fishing by saying "it is important to be out in the open air," instead of regarding fishing as a pleasure in itself. Here is an example of ends-means relationship with respect to my own children. In Chicago we lived in an apartment with a self-operating elevator. I found that I pushed the button in order to get upstairs; but to my children, pressing the elevator button and releasing the amazing consequences of that act was a pleasure in itself, to be undertaken leisurely, zestfully, and with sparkling eyes. So it used to take us a long time to get upstairs. The point is that self-actualizing people, like children, enjoy as ends in themselves hundreds of little things that to ordinary people are only means.

Rogers says of the same point, "Such living in the moment means an absence of rigidity, of tight organization, of the imposition of a structure. It means, instead, a maximum of adaptability, a discovery of structure in experience, of a flowing, changing organization of the self and of personality rather than the imposition of structure upon experience."

Another characteristic of the fully functioning personality is that he is a creative individual, sometimes creative in the usual sense of being an artist, musician, novelist, scientist, or political leader, but just as often creative in smaller, but equally genuine, ways, in the ability of the carpenter, the office manager, the house-organ editor, the housewife, or the teacher to improvise, for the particular needs of a job at hand, out of the particular materials at hand, a unique and original solution of a problem, a solution that immediately strikes others with a thrill of pleasure, so that they say, "How did you ever think of that!" This is what I mean by creativeness.

Maslow writes that there are no exceptions to the rule that self-actualizing people are all creative in their own way.

Rogers says that in a creative person, and therefore a fully functioning person, "the locus of evaluation is in the self." It isn't what teachers think, it isn't what the Ph.D. committee thinks, it isn't what the neighbors think, it's what *I* think. Because the fully functioning person's experiences, past and present, are accessible to awareness, because he sees freshly and without rigid categorizing or labeling of the situation before him, he ultimately is his own judge of what is the needed solution for any given problem. After all, the solutions of others are merely the solutions of people who weren't in *this* situation, confronted with *this* problem with *these* materials or with *these* people to work with. Therefore, the fully functioning person, even if he may welcome the praise or admiration of others, is not dependent on others.

Perhaps from this we can give an account in general semantics terms of the creative process. Let me put it something like this: if you see in any given situation only what everybody else can see, you can be said to be so much a representative of your culture that you are a victim of it. In other words, you haven't even got the materials to be original with, since you have before you only just another sunset, just another tree, just another batch of leftovers in the icebox— these are the common abstractions. But if you are extensional about the world around you, open to the uniqueness of every object and event, if you are open, too, about your own feelings, namely, the uniqueness of your tensions and needs at this moment, and of those around you, what is before you is not just another sunset, or just another tree, or just another batch of leftovers. And the act of bringing together the uniqueness of yourself at that moment with the uniqueness of your materials at that moment and the uniqueness of other people's feelings at that moment to solve a problem is the act of creativity: whether the end-product takes the form of a painting, a sonata, a plan for prison reform, or a new kind of casserole dish.

What D. H. Lawrence says about art seems to me to be what Maslow and Rogers say about the completed relationship of a genuinely sane person and his world.

"The business of art is to reveal the relation between man and his circumambient universe, at this living moment. As mankind is always struggling in the toil of old relationships, art is always ahead of its 'times', which themselves are always far in the rear of the living present.

"When van Gogh paints sunflowers, he reveals, or achieves, the vivid relationship between himself, as man, and the sunflower, as sunflower, at that quick moment of time. His painting is not the sunflower itself. We shall never know what the sunflower is. The camera will visualize the sunflower far more perfectly than van Gogh ever did.

"The vision on the canvas is a third thing, utterly intangible and inexplicable, the offspring of the sunflower itself and van Gogh himself. The vision on the canvas is forever incommensurable with the canvas, or the paint, or van Gogh as a human organism, or the sunflower as a botanical organism. You cannot weigh nor measure nor even describe the vision on the canvas. . . .

"It is a revelation of a perfected relation, at a certain moment, between man and a sunflower . . . and this perfected relation between man and his circumambient universe is life itself, for mankind. . . . Man and the sunflower both pass away in a moment, in the process of forming a new relationship. The relation between all things changes from day to day, in a subtle stealth of change. Hence art, which reveals or attains to another perfect relationship, will be for ever new.

"If we think about it, we find that our life consists in this achieving of a pure relationship between ourselves and the living universe about us. This is how I 'save my soul' by accomplishing a pure relationship between me and another person, me and other people, me and a nation, me and a race of men, me and animals, me and the trees or flowers, me and the earth, me and the skies and sun and stars, me and the moon: an infinity of pure relations, big and little. . . . This, if we knew it, is our life and our eternity: the subtle, perfected relation between me and the circumambient universe."

Finally, the fully functioning personality is ethical in the deepest sense. Maslow says that his sane people have a sense of right and wrong that is quite clear cut, but that their evaluations are at deeper levels, rather than at the superficial levels that most people worry about. He says that ordinary "moral" problems fade out of existence for sane people. "It is not so much that the problem is solved as that it becomes clearly seen that it never was an intrinsic problem to start with, but it was only a sick-man-created one, e.g., whether or not one plays cards or dances, or wears short or long dresses, exposing the head in some churches and covering it in others, drinking wine, eating some meats and not others, or eating them on some days and not others."

For the fully functioning personality, these problems are deflated. Rogers says on the same point that because the fully functioning personality is nondefensive, and because he therefore has access to his own needs and those of others, he can be counted on to be trustworthy and constructive. That is, the unsane individual is moral only with the greatest of effort, and often he behaves unmorally and viciously with the best of moral intentions, whereas to the fully functioning personality, as Rogers, Maslow, and Korzybski see him, morality and ethics come naturally, as the result of proper evaluation. A person who is fully open to his own feelings and deeply aware of other people as well, can hardly act blindly or selfishly. He is deeply socialized, as Rogers says, because "one of his own deepest needs is for affiliation and communication with others. When he is most fully himself—'selfish'—he cannot help but be most deeply identified with others too and therefore his orientation is social in the best sense." But the anxious and the fearful and the neurotic person is moral only with effort; because of his lack of self-insight, he hurts others when he does not intend to.

This picture of the sane person may sound like an impossible ideal. I don't want it to sound that way. What is the sane person like to meet? What does he look like? Well, he (or she) may be short or tall, may be thin or fat. He (or she) may wear false teeth or have fallen arches or bifocals. He (or she) may be childlike in some respects and therefore may appear childish to his friends and neighbors. Because he is somewhat detached from his culture, he may seem cold and distant to others. But, most importantly, this sane person that I have been describing may suffer from anxiety and fear and doubt and foreboding—because such feelings can arise from non-neurotic sources in this troubled world—so that externally he (or she) may look just as troubled and act just as troubled as a neurotic person. But his troubles would be real ones and not self-contrived ones.

I say this last because sometimes we speak of the goals of mental health as if they meant the hope of the emergence of completely happy people in a completely trouble-free world. If such were our goal, it would indeed be impossible and unattainable. Actually, it seems to me that the goals of mental health are much more modest. Sanity does not mean the solution of all problems (cultural or political or economic or whatever), but merely the abolition or avoidance of those problems we create for ourselves through lack of self-insight. And self-insight is necessary and prior to all other kinds of insight.

VI

THE SELF-IMAGE AND INTERCULTURAL

UNDERSTANDING, OR HOW TO

BE SANE THOUGH NEGRO

IT would seem the utmost effrontery on my part to write on the subject of the psychological problems of being Negro. I am not a Negro, and, as they used to say before congressional committees, never have been.

But, while I am not a Negro, I am a member of a minority group—one that has been the victim of a certain amount of discrimination and prejudice, sometimes even persecution. I have had to wrestle with some of the same problems the Negro must confront, although no doubt in attenuated form. I was advised in my youth, for example, that there were many jobs and careers I could not hope to aspire to because of my race. Especially during the sensitive years of late adolescence, I met social rebuffs (or imagined rebuffs) which caused me to suffer at least some of the inward torture that Negroes in a mixed society must suffer. In later years, after I had decided to be trained as a writer and teacher of English, I saw what I thought were dozens of people with smaller abilities than my own getting jobs while I cooled my heels in the graduate school waiting for an opening, and wondering if I was being discriminated against. Paranoid feelings and paranoia itself are the constant pitfalls of minority-group psychology. So I can lay claim to some firsthand acquaintance with how it feels to be one of a minority group; and even if I was not sent to a Japanese relocation center during the war years, I felt intensely the meaning of that relocation.

Certainly the minority-group identification must have been strong in me during the first months of World War II, because when, in November 1942, I was invited to become a weekly columnist of the Chicago *Defender,* I accepted with pleasure. I continued that column until the end of 1946, and during that time I acquired an emotional identification with the Negro world, which I still retain. Much of what I write develops from what I felt and saw among my Negro friends and acquaintances in the course of the professional and social life I led in the Negro community in Chicago and elsewhere from the moment I began to work for the *Defender.*

But more importantly, as a student of general semantics, I find that this discipline throws an enormous amount of light upon the problems that all of us, of whatever race, have in achieving adjustment and self-realization in this extremely complex and rapidly changing world of the twentieth century.

Let me start off with the explanation of a semantic principle: the self-fulfilling prophecy.

A self-fulfilling prophecy is one that fulfills itself as the result of the behavior of the person who makes the prophecy and believes it. Suppose we hear a rumor that the bank in which we all have our money is about to fail. Suppose that we all believe the rumor *and act upon it,* so that we all rush to the bank to get our money out. This is exactly what causes bank failures. Or, take another example: here is a young man just out of jail who is looking for a job. Let us suppose that no one in town will give him a job because of his past record. In other words, those who refuse to employ him are making a prediction that since the young man has erred in the past, he will err again. Ultimately, the young man, unable to get an honest job anywhere, returns to crime. When he is caught again, people are likely to say, "See? What did I tell you? A criminal is always a criminal." But the doubt remains: was it not the unanimous prediction that he *would* return to crime that caused him to return to crime?

But the self-fulfilling prophecy has its benign aspects as well as its unfortunate ones. An acquaintance of mine, upon his release from prison, got a job as handy man in an elegant shop on Michigan Avenue in Chicago. After a few days on the job his employer gave him eight hundred dollars in cash to take to the bank. In other words, the employer was making the prediction, "This man can be trusted." I have seen my friend frequently in the six years since this happened. He is still working in the same store, but he is a new and different man. He is not only a responsible man; he is accepting more and more responsibilities. His employer's prediction is being fulfilled twentyfold.

I am not saying that such prophecies always fulfill themselves, because that would be a manifest absurdity. But what I am saying is that *your own beliefs about the outcome of any social situation of which you are a part are a factor in the outcome.* You have heard white people who say, "If Negroes move into our community, there is bound to be trouble." You know that, although such people believe they are stating an impersonal fact, there is an enormous personal element in such statements; in other words, you sense that they themselves are, subtly or unsubtly, going to help make that trouble.

But the mechanism of the self-fulfilling prophecy works the other way, too. If a Negro goes into mixed company with the prediction inside him that "People are going to be unpleasant to me because of my race," they may very well be unpleasant to him. Later, he will say, "I told you so," and regard himself complacently as a realist who was able accurately to foresee the situation.

There is the consciously uttered self-fulfilling prophecy, such as "We *will* achieve our sales quota!" and "There'll *always* be an England!" which, if believed with enough ardor, helps people to achieve their quotas or to save England. But even more important from my point of view are the prophecies *unconsciously* made which reveal themselves in ways of which we may be completely unaware. To cite an extreme case, the dog that has often been kicked reveals, in the very way it slinks down the street, the fact that it expects to be kicked again—so that some feel an almost irresistible temptation to give him another kick as he goes by.

The expectations we have of life—in other words, the conscious or unconscious prophecies we make about how other people are going to treat us—are the combined product of our experience, our education, and our miseducation. We have all had vast amounts of assorted experiences; we have all been subjected to vast amounts of assorted education and miseducation, from our parents, teachers, newspapers, preachers, television, movies, radio, literature, and drama, all of which purport to tell us something about life, or segments of life. Also, our experiences are filtered through our education or miseducation, so that out of the same events, different people learn entirely different things: for example, from similar experiences with pretty and avaricious women, one man may learn never to have anything more to do with *that particular woman;* another man may learn never to have anything more to do with *any* woman; still another man may learn nothing at all and go back for more. Hence, the kind of persons we are today reflects not only our experiences, but also what we have been able to abstract from them.

All the foregoing are, perhaps, psychological truisms, and there would be no special point in mentioning them were it not for the fact that in this period of changing race relations, all sorts of attitudes once perfectly sensible have suddenly ceased to be altogether realistic. Furthermore, personal sets of expectations—personal attitudes—on the part of both Negroes and whites have recently assumed an altogether unprecedented importance. Twenty years ago, many white people had little or no contact with Negroes, and many Negroes had little or no contact with whites. People really lived in a more severely segregated world than we now do in urban centers throughout the United States. Therefore the expectations Negroes had of whites or whites of Negroes, whether favorable or unfavorable, had less practical effect at the level of day-to-day relationships than they have today. Now, however, the number of daily contacts with people of another race is increasing—in school, in public transportation, in business, at sports events, in factories, and in social life. With this steady increase in daily interracial contact, the importance of personal attitudes increases.

I emphasize personal attitudes because in one sense it can be said that the fight for desegregation, and therefore equality, has already been won. Lest this sound like an overstatement, let me explain what I mean. It has been won, first of all, at the level of the Supreme Court and federal law. It has also been won at the level of mass communications; no national magazine, no radio or television network, no press syndicate, no newspaper outside of the South, neither major political party, questions any longer the right of Negroes to full participation in the rights and privileges of being Americans. Even Southerners who subscribe to the "separate-but-equal" doctrine are at least verbally in agreement with the principle of equality. Those who really believe that Negroes are not entitled to equal rights constitute a minority—indeed, except for a few in Congress, a partially frustrated and extremely defensive minority, since they have almost no access to sympathetic presentation of their views in the mass media. This situation may well constitute, as some Southerners charge, an abridgment of freedom of speech. But it does show that equality, as a moral principle, is almost universally established.

Hence the battleground for equal rights—at least for those in the North and West—is no longer predominantly in the courts or in legislatures. It is largely in the field of personal relations—which immediately makes obsolete the whole concept of "battleground." To be sure, there remains a vast amount of work to be done before equality is established in fact as well as in principle. If there is not legal segregation in the North and West, there is still unofficial, or bootleg, segregation on a grand scale, through the gerrymandering of school districts and other methods, the most important of which is the control of real estate. These facts reveal the dividedness, the ambivalence, in the hearts of most white people: they simultaneously want Negroes to get ahead because they genuinely believe that equality is desirable, and they don't want Negroes to get ahead because they might find Negroes as their next-door neighbors. This ambivalence in the hearts of most white people places an unprecedented power and opportunity in Negro hands. It is this power and opportunity that I wish to discuss.

More and more often, as segregation breaks down, Negroes find themselves among a larger group of whites. Since many white people, either because of unfamiliarity or because of the ambivalence I have already mentioned, are uncertain how to behave in an interracial situation, they unconsciously look to the Negro for guidance. In other words, the Negro, to a degree hitherto impossible, can set the tone of social or business intercourse by the clues he gives in his speech and behavior as to how he expects to be treated.

Because the Negro is in such a strategic position in situations of interracial contact, the kind of self-image or self-concept he possesses becomes a matter of crucial importance. An important ingredient of the self-image of the Negro is simply the statement "I am a Negro." Such a statement, like other perceptions of the self ("I am a United States Marine," "I am a high-school teacher," "I am a Ph.D., "I am not a Ph.D."), may be accompanied by feelings of pride or satisfaction, embarrassment or shame. Or it may be a simple statement of fact, accompanied by no special feelings one way or the other.

If the self-concept "I am a Negro" is accompanied by feelings of inferiority introjected from traditional white evaluations, the Negro will act obsequiously, as if he expected to be stepped on—and he will find many white people only too willing to oblige. If it is accompanied by feelings of defensiveness, as if he expected to be treated rudely because he is Negro, he is likely to arouse a counter-defensiveness in whites. If, however, the perception "I am a Negro" is felt only as a simple statement of fact, with few or no affective components one way or the other, the Negro will act naturally, and white people will, in nine cases out of ten, act naturally, too, and be happy and relieved that meeting a Negro was not the ordeal they thought it was going to be. But however the Negro acts, the power to determine the atmosphere and outcome of the meeting lies with him.

The reader, especially if he is Negro, can probably think of instances in his own experience where "acting naturally" did no good. I am willing to grant that there are situations in which it will do no good. But I also wish to offer a counter-challenge, namely, how do you know you acted naturally? This brings me to the crux of the theory of the self-fulfilling prophecy.

What does it mean to "act naturally"? Let us put this expression back into the context of a living situation to see what it means. Let us say that you have entertained at your home some extremely exalted or famous person—maybe a movie star or the Prime Minister of England. Let us say that this person proved to be an altogether pleasant guest, who made himself so much one of the family at your home that he put everybody at his ease. Your way of expressing your pleasure would be to say, "He just seemed like one of us, he acted so naturally!" And another way of stating this fact would be: Your distinguished guest, instead of constantly reminding you that he was a movie star or the Prime Minister of England, and demanding special consideration on that account, reacted without affectation to you, your home, your friends, your children, so that you felt at ease with him. If, on the other hand, he hadn't "acted naturally"—if he had constantly reminded you of his special position and his great fame—you would have said after he had gone, "Well, I'm glad *that's* over!" The secret of acting naturally, if you are a movie star or the Prime Minister of England, is to forget that you are a movie star or the Prime Minister of England.

What I should like to point out is that being a Negro in a mixed society is exactly the same kind of problem. The secret of acting naturally, and therefore of how to be sane though Negro, is to forget as far as possible that one is Negro. If you are a biochemist and this fact is foremost in your self-image, you will expect to be treated as just another biochemist; the self-fulfilling prophecy will operate, and people will in all likelihood treat you as just another biochemist. If you are a parent and expect to be treated as just another parent at a P.-T.A. meeting, people will in all likelihood treat you as just another parent, learning, meanwhile, that the problems of Negro parents are no different from those of white parents. But if you are a biochemist or a parent and expect to be treated as a Negro, people are going to treat you as a Negro—whatever that means to them.

But, you will say, that is easier said than done. How can we submerge or forget the fact of being Negroes when the white world keeps reminding us over and over again, with Jim Crow signs, with residential restrictions, with job discrimination, with special forms of rudeness, and even with special forms of exaggerated politeness? Again I grant that the questions are just. It is not easy to forget.

However, difficult as forgetting is, it is precisely the problem that must be tackled. The reason for this is that the standard complaint of Negroes is, as a student of mine expressed it in an essay, "I'm tired of being regarded as something special. I'm tired of being 'Colored' or 'Negro.' I'm tired of being a symbol of a whole race. I'm just me and I want to be treated as such." But notice here again the operation of the self-fulfilling prophecy. If you want to be treated as "just me," you've got to think of yourself as "just me," and not as "me, a Negro." So in reply to the Negro who says, "I'd be glad to forget, if only they'd let me," I would say, "Most of them would just as soon forget, too, but they must learn from you how to do it."

The difficulty of "forgetting," however, is mitigated considerably by the fact that neither "remember" nor "forget" are absolute terms. It is no more necessary to forget absolutely than it is to be haunted by the fact of being Negro all day long. What is necessary, with society and social conditions as they are today, is to remember only when one has to remember, and to forget the rest of the time. And what is important to keep in mind is that the occasions on which one has to remember are constantly being reduced—for that is exactly what nonsegregation means.

I want to emphasize the fact that times are changing,

faster than most of us realize. It is hard to realize the rapidity of the changes because, at the level of words, white Southerners are writing the same kind of speeches they have uttered for the past twenty years about "the unalterable traditions of the South." On the other side the National Association for the Advancement of Colored People and the Negro newspapers and the Negro spokesmen, with their attention fixed on how much farther there is to go rather than how far we have come, continue to give the same angry speeches and write the same fiery editorials that they have for the past twenty years. At the level of words, I repeat, thing *sound* pretty much the same as they did twenty years ago.

At the level of facts, however, hundreds of thousands of ordinary people, white and Negro, who twenty years ago used to lunch separately, are now eating together in factory lunchrooms, school cafeterias, hamburger stands, dining cars, and other places of public refreshment. But the trouble with an uneventful lunch at which whites and Negroes manage to get down their blue-plate specials without having a riot, is that it can never get into the papers. It is, in a curious way, a wordless experience—people simply eat their lunches and pay their checks, and the national offices of neither the NAACP nor the Ku Klux Klan get any word of it. Across the country, thousands of white and Negro students are helping each other with their homework, thousands of white and Negro housewives and their children are meeting at common playgrounds and talking with each other, thousands of white and Negro men and women are working together in committees, in factories, and in offices, who, twenty years ago, would not even have come in contact with each other. Very little of this gets into the papers, because of a fundamental journalistic fact: if 9,999 automobiles make a safe journey home after a Fourth of July weekend, it is only the ten thousandth car, which smashed up, that gets into the news.

It is necessary, then, for a Negro or a member of any other minority group to take equality for granted and go on from there. How can we achieve this state of mind?

Let me quote again from a student paper. The student complains about such incidents as the following. First, a white salesman in a clothing store, impressed by the student's good English, asked if he was a doctor. The student replied angrily, "I want you to know that Negro doctors and professional men are not the only Negroes who talk intelligently!" Again, the student expresses himself as infuriated by such remarks by whites as "I've always felt very kindly and sympathetic toward your people." He writes, "That remark, well meant, I know, usually spoils life for a few minutes and makes me feel as if I'm at someone's funeral. At other times my feelings reach the other extreme and I have the urge to shout, 'Who the hell are my people?'" This student also is bitter about the kind of person who asks, "You don't happen to know Wilbur Atkins, do you? A real nice fellow—used to be porter at Hale's."

It appears to me that if one takes equality for granted, there is nothing especially offensive in any of these remarks. They reveal naïveté on the part of the whites who make them. They are, nevertheless, as the student admits, "well meant"; they are clumsy and graceless attempts to establish some kind of contact. Lillian Smith says that on the subject of Negroes most white people are ignorant, blind, and sick. Many Negro writers have said the same thing. Hence, in reply to the student, I must ask in turn: Why get angry with these poor, ignorant, sick people who are trying to be friendly? Why not give them a C-minus for effort and forget it? How much enlightenment do you expect from white people with the kind of education on the subject of Negroes that most of them have had—education in terms of the clichés of minstrel shows, bad vaudeville jokes, movie and radio and television and newspaper comic stereotypes, and superstitious folklore? If you expect too much of them—if you expect all white people to be intelligent and sensible on the subject of Negroes—you will be running into daily disappointments. If, however, your expectations are realistic—in other words, if you expect four out of five white persons to be pretty ignorant on the subject—then you will be delighted when the score for a given day turns out to be only three out of five.

Korzybski used to talk about "minimum expectation" as the basis of happiness. The following is my own example of the principle. Years ago I used to notice the differences among motormen on the Indiana Avenue streetcar line in Chicago—a street often blocked by badly parked cars and huge trailer trucks backing into warehouses and maneuvering in everybody's way. Some motormen seemed to expect to be able to drive down Indiana Avenue without interruption. Every time they got blocked, they would get steamed up with rage, clang their bells and lean out of their cars to shout at the truck drivers. At the end of a day these motormen must have been nervous wrecks; I can imagine them coming home at the end of a day, jittery and hypertensive, a menace to their wives and children. Other motormen, however, seemed to expect Indiana Avenue to be heavily blocked—a realistic expectation, because it usually was. They could sit and wait for minutes without impatience, calmly whistling a tune, cleaning their fingernails, or writing their reports. In other words, confronting the same objective situation, some motormen lived a hellish life of anger and nervous tension; other motormen had a nice, relaxing job, with plenty of time for rest.

Every instance on natural communication between Negro and white in which racial consciousness is truly absent can be, for the white person who needs it, a kind of psychotherapy —and goodness knows most white people need it. I call it a form of psychotherapy because through it the individual learns to react appropriately, which is to say, not to the color of the speaker's skin, but to what he is saying. Wendell Johnson writes, "A speaker whose skin happens to be relatively dark, so that his listeners classify him—more or less irrelevantly—as a Negro, can speak great wisdom only to have it fall on deaf ears. . . . Any kind of prejudice, racial or not, tends to result in a sort of functional deafness." If whites are to learn how to get over their prevailing obsession with skin color, they must learn how from Negroes who themselves are unobsessed—with their own skin color or anyone else's. In this insane situation of race relations, Negroes must act as the white man's psychotherapist.

Communication, however, is an interactional—a transactional—process. Insofar as Negroes help white persons become more sane, white persons in their turn will help Negroes become more sane—and goodness knows Negroes need psychotherapy in this matter too, since skin color, especially their own, has been a limiting and circumscribing factor every day of their lives.

Accurate and undistorted perceptions of the self are a necessary condition to accuracy in all other perceptions. To permit the self-perception "I am a Negro" to dominate and condition and limit all other self-perceptions is perhaps the most insidious form of Jim Crow. I should like to call it "Jim Crow of the mind." Physical Jim Crow is imposed by others —by fences, barricades, "white" and "colored" signs over drinking fountains. But Jim Crow of the mind is not that which is enforced by headwaiters, employment agencies, railroad companies, or the police. It is that which limits the perspective of all too many Negro students to studies of Negro literature, Negro art, Negro sociology, Negro history. Teachers all too often encourage this mental Jim Crow by assigning Negro topics to their Negro students.

If you look at the titles of dissertations in the graduate

divisions of Negro universities, you will note the widespread existence of this Jim Crow of the mind—dissertations on Negro housing, Negro population movements, Negro journalism, Negro poetry, and so on indefinitely. Granted that some of these dissertations are justified by the exigencies of research in particular localities, the almost total absence of topics not limited to the Negro is a depressing commentary on the one-sidedness of academic life in many Negro colleges.

But these students are by no means unusual. Let us look at the community of educated, upper-middle-class Negroes. Are they seriously interested in music, or do they go to concerts only when Marian Anderson or Leontyne Price is singing? Are they genuinely interested in art, or do they only go to art shows when Jacob Lawrence or Eldizir Cortor is exhibiting? Are they really interested in sociology, or only in the sociology of the Negro? (Incidentally, Negroes are not alone in this kind of self-limitation. I know of a Chinese-American professor of sociology who is an authority on Chinatowns in the United States and practically never talks about anything else.)

I do not blame anyone for this intellectual segregation, which is the inevitable product of the history of Negroes in the United States. But what is past is past. Hence the question I am raising is whether the removal of Jim Crow of the mind is keeping pace with the removal of physical Jim Crow. Is it not possible that we are carrying into the present attitudes and habits which, while once appropriate and necessary, are now partly antiquated?

Long after a national fair-employment-practices law is on the books, long after the last segregated schoolhouse in the United States is abolished, we shall still have to reckon with Jim Crow of the mind. Because it is an inner problem, it is not one that Negroes can solve simply by blaming everything on the whites. Because it is an inner problem, it is for each individual a personal responsibility.

The way to stop being haunted by the memory of a girl who jilted you is to get a new girl. The way to stop being haunted by the fact of being Negro, which is the essence of Jim Crow of the mind, is to develop a deeper passion about other topics. Let me suggest some methods.

First, I believe every Negro should interest himself, not superficially, but deeply, in the problems of some minority other than his own. The study of the problems of Italian immigrants or of the Jews is good for Negroes, in the same way that the study of Negroes is good for the Italians and the Jews. But there are minority groups other than ethnic to be studied: the stutterers, the physically handicapped, the blind, and the members of all sorts of other social minorities who develop their own minority-group complexes. The more intensively one studies any such group, the more impressive become the similarities among all human beings. Read the history of the Irish under English oppression, and study in the light of that history the characteristic fears, prejudices, aggressions, and ancient loyalties that still distinguish many American descendants of those Irish four or five generations later. Gradually, as we pursue such studies, we begin to lose the sense of a special "Negro problem," just as I have long ago lost the sense of a special "Japanese problem," and we acquire instead a sense of the profound similarity of all human problems.

My next suggestion has specifically to do with the younger generation. I do not believe a student should be advised to give up any plans, schooling, or future aspirations simply on the basis of being a Negro. The fate of an earlier generation of Negroes who trained to be electrical engineers and had to accept employment as Pullman porters has led many to caution young people against training for jobs beyond those which they believe a Negro can get. I think it is of utmost importance today to re-examine this point of view. There is no doubt still a job ceiling, but it is neither as low as it used to be nor as rigid, and insofar as it exists, it has only the sanction of custom, and not that of law.

If a group of Negro students say to themselves, "There's no use studying to become an electrical engineer because we'll never get jobs," they will obviously never get to be engineers. If, on the other hand, they say to themselves, "We shall become electrical engineers, come hell or high water," they will at least have the training to push against the job ceiling, and some of them may break through and fulfill their own prophecies. It's a gamble, of course, and they may lose and wind up as Pullman porters after all. But it is less of a gamble today than it was in 1949, and in 1969 it will be still less of a gamble, because of the steady changes that we have all seen going on. Job ceilings cannot be broken by legislation alone, because not even a fair-employment-practices law can compel the hiring of a nonengineer for an engineer's job. So an increasing number of young men and women today must be encouraged to take a long chance and train themselves for positions which Negroes have never held before. The basic question facing a young man or woman today in the choice of a career is not "Is this career open to Negroes?"—a question that reflects the very essence of Jim Crow of the mind. It is, rather, "Is this career one that I care about enough to try for?" Courageous young men and women, by acting as if there were equality of opportunity, will, by the terms of the self-fulfilling prophecy, bring about the equality of opportunity that they seek.

That last sentence, I am afraid, sounds inspirational. It is all very well to tell people to be courageous, but, as a student of semantics, I know that preaching is not enough. Hence, I should like to explain in semantic terms what being courageous means.

I believe that what we call courage is nothing more than what general semanticists call being "extensional." Being extensional means constantly being on the lookout for changes and differences in events and things and people that we would otherwise evaluate as unchanged. The basic principles of extensionality are the extremely simple indexing and dating: Korzybski's rule that $chair_1$ is not $chair_2$ is not $chair_3$ . . . and Mr. $Jones_{1960}$ is not Mr. $Jones_{1962}$ is not Mr. $Jones_{1964}$. The person who maintains this fluidity of concept in terms of time is always on the alert for altered conditions, which may mean altered opportunities. He is also aware that he himself is changing from day to day, month to month, and year to year, so that he has constantly to reassess his strengths, abilities, and attitudes.

The extensional person is relatively courageous, then, not because he is foolhardy, but because he knows that the things he has been afraid of have changed, that he himself has changed, so that the future is always in some respects, for better or worse, different from the past. Therefore, past fears inevitably have less meaning for the extensional person than curiosity about the future. Adjusted to change and difference, the extensional person seems often to walk in where angels fear to tread, not because he is a fool, but because he has been curious enough to investigate what it was the angels were afraid of—and has discovered that whatever it was, it isn't there any more. Without the habit of indexing and dating, one would not have bothered to investigate; one would simply have taken the angels' word for it. In other words, the person who indexes his judgments does not conclude, because the Snowhite Corporation of Minneapolis refused him a job, that the Snowhite Corporation of Kansas City will necessarily do the same. The person who dates his opinions has no airtight conclusions about the present state of affairs in the restaurant where he was refused service in 1961. For the extensional person the world is never dull—it is vivid with potentialities. If he hears that such-and-such a firm does not hire Negroes, he will reply, "But they haven't seen me yet." After they've seen him, he may still be without a job. But the mere fact of his applying may start within the firm a discussion of whether or not they should hire Negroes—a discussion that in many firms has not even begun, because no Negro has ever applied.

I write as I do because, despite Governor Wallace and his supporters, I believe that in the long struggle for equality of rights and opportunities, Negroes simply cannot lose. The moral sense of the nation (except in a few pockets of resistance), economic conditions, technological necessities, historical social forces both here and abroad, and, most importantly, the practical necessities of living together in our extremely close-knit and interdependent economy will compel the end of enforced segregation, both official and unofficial. Sylvia Porter has written in her syndicated column that industries planning to build new plants in Alabama and Georgia were changing their minds, much to the consternation of local chambers of commerce, because of the racial situation. Hopes of industrial development in Arkansas were at the time severely set back by events in Little Rock. Hence, from within Southern business circles there is apparently a mounting pressure on the segregationists to desist, because racial antagonism is going to cost too much money. If Negroes counter violence with passive resistance, as has been the policy since the bus boycotters of Montgomery, Alabama, never descending to or condoning violence themselves, if they continue to use the power of the law itself, as is the policy of the NAACP, progress is inevitable. If tactical errors are going to be made out of anxiety and fear, let the segregationists make them, as they continue to do by harassing peaceful demonstrators with electric cattle prods and police dogs, burning Negro homes, harassing Negro children, and otherwise destroying, through violent and often illegal actions, any pretensions they may cherish as to the moral basis of their position.

So we come, finally, to the greatest of social prophecies, the self-fulfilling prophecy of political democracy. It is a prophecy that fulfills itself slowly, not only because it is a huge one that takes a lot of fulfilling, but also because all of us, white and Negro and all the shades between, have faltered in our belief in it and have lacked the faith always to act upon it. The prophecy of democracy states that if we indeed treat each other as created equal and therefore act on the principle of respect for all persons regardless of race, color, religion, or previous condition of servitude, we shall all of us—both the oppressors and the oppressed—be healed of the profound emotional scars that we inherit from earlier and less just forms of human organization, and attain full human dignity. Like all self-fulfilling prophecies, this prophecy will not fulfill itself on the dawn of a sudden Day of Jubilee. It fulfills itself only as we accept its premises, accept the responsibilities it places on each of us individually, and prepare ourselves, not to fight over again the battles of yesterday, but to take our places, with pride and dignity, in the changed world of tomorrow.

VII

STATUS₁, STATUS₂, STATUS₃

IN *The Status Seekers,* Vance Packard gives a rapid and readable account of social classes in America. If, as is quite unlikely, you imagine that America is a truly equalitarian society, you will be shocked at the revelation of the extent of class differences. If, however, whether as headwaiter, society leader, sociologist, or amateur observer, you already know about class differences, you will recognize the truth of much that the author says, and you will derive new information besides, because he has surveyed a vast amount of literature in preparing this book.

The author divides American society into two main classes, roughly comparable to officers and enlisted men, the "diploma elite" and the "supporting classes." The former are divided into the "real upper class" and the "semi-upper class." The latter he divides into the "limited-success class," the "working class" and the "real lower class." He calls the upper group the "diploma elite" to underline the fact that, in the main, the biggest division in our society is that between those who have gone to college and those who have not.

The great change Packard finds in the class structure of today as compared, for example, with Middletown of the 1920's as studied by Robert S. and Helen Merrell Lynd is that whereas formerly the great division was between the white-collar and blue-collar classes, today the skilled and unionized worker is economically and socially equal to and often well above a large proportion of white-collar workers. The author therefore places skilled workers and the lower levels of white-collar workers together in what he calls the "limited-success class"—the skilled worker being limited because he is doing well and doesn't want to go further, the low-paid white-collar worker being limited because he can't go further. These together, the top level of the "supporting classes," are the warrant officers and sergeants of society.

Packard's most serious charge against present-day America is that it has become virtually impossible to start at the bottom as "private" and get to the top as "general." To become a "general" at all, one has to start as "lieutenant," *i.e.*, college graduate. This is the most important particular of his general charge that American social structure is showing dangerous signs of freezing, contrary to our cherished American belief in equality of opportunity for all.

The author ascribes this freezing of our class structure (taking due account of tendencies in the opposite direction) to a number of causes. The bigness of big business, resulting in increased bureaucratization, is one cause. For example, it is easier in large organizations to demand a college diploma as minimum qualification for executive training than to sift through the rank and file for hidden talent. Automation and specialization are further causes. Routine machine-tending and minute division of labor give the individual worker little chance to understand the whole of the process in which a factory is engaged, and therefore gives him no chance to move up from the assembly line. Many of the "steppingstone" positions between the assembly line and the executive office have disappeared. Unions, by insisting on promotion by seniority and by opposing the free movement of workers from job to job in a plant, also discourage those who would like to try to break into the "officer class." Furthermore, Packard charges, in the society outside one's place of business there is "the growing tendency for people to confine their socializing to their own socio-economic layer." There is also "stratification by residential area," much encouraged by tract housing, which enforces social grouping not only by income level, but also by race.

Many of Packard's contentions are sound, and I applaud his wish that the doors to college education, and therefore the higher opportunity, be opened more generously to the "supporting classes," who have among them proportionately as many children of high intelligence as the "diploma elite." And it is important to assess, as Packard does, the impact of technologies—automation in factories, mass production in housing—on social structure.

Nevertheless, *The Status Seekers* is an exasperating book. It is exasperating in part because of something inherent in sociology: its tendency to prove through solemn surveys what are matters of common observation—for example, that the children of the educated and the well-to-do have a better chance of achieving eminence than the children of the uneducated and the poor.

Another source of exasperation is the author's ascribing to considerations of social status many things which can be otherwise and more readily explained. For example, he cites a study that shows that juries of mixed social class tend to elect as chairmen and to concur in the judgments of people of high social status, such as proprietors and professional men. But since the task of juries is the evaluation of human behavior and motives and the understanding of laws, is there not a reason more compelling than social status for the influence in juries of those who, by virtue of their daily tasks, have more experience in such evaluation than, say, mechanics or farmers or factory workers?

But the major disappointment in the book is Packard's unclarified ideas about status—although the literature he himself cites could have clarified his ideas had he thought about it longer and harder. There are at least three kinds of status, all of which the author touches upon without distinguishing. The first is status-by-definition. If whites are defined as superior to Negroes, then any white, no matter how shiftless and ignorant, is superior to any Negro, no matter how talented and useful. Then there is status-by-consumption, in terms of which Bill is superior to Joe if Bill has a handsomer car, a more expensive house, or a more fashionable suit of clothes than Joe can display. Finally there is status-by-achievement, in which that individual is regarded as superior who, in his chosen line of endeavor, does a better job than others: the ballplayer who hits .375 or the scientist who solves a previously insoluble problem.

Because he has not clarified his concepts of status, Packard sounds as if he thinks that status seeking is something wicked in itself, although what he clearly desires is a society in which achievement is the principal measure of status. He fails to point out that *both* status-by-consumption *and* status-by-achievement run *counter to* status-by-definition. In a world of status-by-definition, you can't go up or down.

Since status-by-achievement is open only to the talented minority, and since we all need some sense of status, the widespread practice, much encouraged by advertising, of seeking status-by-consumption is evidence that the dynamism of an open society is still very much at work in America, rather than evidence to the contrary. Moreover, status is not a thing, but an evaluation. Therefore, if a man *thinks* that he has status because he's got a big, long, new car, he *has* status. We may if we wish quarrel with his primitive sense of values. But Packard overlooks the possibility that America's addiction to conspicuous consumption is evidence of the immature strength, rather than the decay, of the American dream.

Packard says that "status seekers are altering our society by their preoccupation, in the midst of plenty, with acquiring evidence of status." A clearer insight into the relation between democracy and abundance is offered by David M. Potter, in *People of Plenty*, who argues that whereas European equalitarianism "is prone to demand that the man of property be stripped of his carriage and fine clothes," the characteristic American demand is that "the ordinary man is entitled to mass-produced copies" of things that formerly only the rich could enjoy. Which is why Chevrolets have become indistinguishable from Cadillacs. And which is also why both will recede in importance as status competition moves to other areas of consumption.

VIII

PROPAGANDA OR INFORMATION?

PROFESSOR William R. Catton has called attention in an article in *ETC.* to an ambiguity which I had not noticed in the general semanticist's use of the term "signal reaction." I am grateful to him for his criticism. If you want help with your luggage at a railroad station, he writes, aren't you entitled to hail *anyone* dressed like a redcap without bothering about the possible differences between $redcap_1$, $redcap_2$, and $redcap_3$? Does not life in organized society require a certain number of more or less routine, unreflective, "signal reaction" responses? Furthermore, would it be feasible to try to give people all the information they need to make intelligent choices in, say, consumer goods or politics? General semanticists look askance at advertising and propaganda because they produce signal reactions, but insofar as few of us have the time or inclination to collect sufficient facts about toothpastes or candidates to make an intelligent choice, is not the narrowing of choice provided by the affective symbols of advertising and propaganda necessary to the efficient conduct of affairs in modern society?

I agree that the moment one wants help with his luggage, the differences between redcap$_1$ and redcap$_2$ are not a matter of concern. One goes through the routinized procedure of summoning any redcap available because he is a redcap—or is dressed like one. I am sorry that by my previous use of the term "signal reaction" I created the impression that routinized or habitual behavior is to be deplored, as William R. Catton said I had in *Language in Action*. I freely acknowledge that cultures must have patterns of behavior and designations of role if they are to be cultures at all. What I mean by "signal reactions" (and what I probably should have said earlier) are *reactions inappropriate to the situation at hand because of failure to make differentiations which, in that situation, are both relevant and necessary.* In other words, if you want to get your luggage *back* when you get to your taxi, you will no longer be content with any redcap, since only one of them has your luggage. People to whom "all Negroes look alike" can waste a lot of time in a crowded railroad station.

But there are other implications in Catton's article that disturb me. For example, he quotes without approval or dissent from *Propaganda* by Edward L. Bernays to the effect that "The conscious and intelligent manipulation of the organized habits and opinions of the masses is an important element in democratic society. Those who manipulate this unseen mechanism of society constitute an invisible government which is the true ruling power of our country."

If "an invisible government" is "the true ruling power in our country," how can it be called a "democratic society"? Such is not understanding of "democracy." What Bernays is describing is an oligarchy so skillful that those who are ruled don't know they are being ruled, but imagine that they are ruling themselves. If he wants to call that a "democratic society," he is certainly free to do so. But I am surprised that Catton does not at least raise an eyebrow.

We can react safely and without hesitation, says Catton, to the symbol "Grade A, Pasteurized." I too buy milk so labeled. But I am given no choice in the matter. I have yet to find in any store a milk carton labeled "Grade B." Everything is "Grade A" these days. And "pasteurized" has become a magic word. Beer, I notice, is "pasteurized"—although I never heard of anyone getting tuberculosis or undulant fever from drinking unpasteurized beer. And they've processed and pasteurized the living daylights (and the flavor) out of packaged cheeses, so that they last indefinitely even without refrigeration. In other words, not even microorganisms want to eat *those* cheeses. Which makes me sure I don't want to eat them either. But apparently they sell well. Face creams, too, are being pasteurized—although what pasteurization does for perfumed mutton fat to put on one's face I can't imagine. And any day now the hucksters will announce a hi-test, antiknock, flight-tested, pasteurized gasoline. They haven't thought of it yet, to be sure, but as soon as they read this article, they'll go right to work on it.

Government grades are established by law in such a way as to stand for certain well-defined social agreements as to the qualities and properties of consumer goods. But those agreements need to be understood if they are to be used intelligently, and routine reactions simply will not do. For example, some people insist on "Grade A" for everything they buy, including canned tomatoes. That grade is given to canned tomatoes that are whole and look beautiful. If you want to make a spaghetti sauce, the wise thing to do is to buy "Grade C," in which the tomatoes, although equally nutritious, are likely to be in pieces. However, the compulsive—those bound by what I call signal reactions—insist on "Grade A" no matter what they are using their canned tomatoes for.

Or take the matter of meat grading. During World War II, if I remember correctly, the meat shortage resulted in a short supply of beef that could be labeled "U.S. Choice" under the standards then prevailing. Consequently, industry pressure was brought to bear on the government to change the definition of "U.S. Choice" so that meats of lower quality could be so labeled. This change was actually brought about —with the result that "U.S. Choice$_{1941}$" is not "U.S. Choice$_{today}$." But most butchers and packers do not use even these revised grades. Most packers avoid altogether the use of U.S. grades on their beef, preferring to label their meats under private (and therefore unverifiable) systems of grading. These private grades always have attractive names: "premium," "first quality," "five star," and so on. They systematically avoid those names upon which public (verifiable) standards have been placed: "Prime," "Choice," "Commercial." If beef is important to you, it is best *not* to have routinized reactions even to the most elegant-sounding names. And if beef is not important to you, it is still necessary, I believe, to be aware of the fact that "Grade A" may or may not mean something. In beef, it doesn't mean anything.

Catton seems to me to pose impossible alternatives on the basis of which to make decisions: either to believe the propaganda or for "each of us independently to gather all the relevant data and to make up our minds before participating in any social decision." As regards canned foods or political candidates, I know I cannot gather all the relevant data. But I don't have to take on faith the utterances of interested propagandists either. The great problem in our culture is not faith versus complete knowledge. It is that of finding *disinterested* sources of information.

There is a limit to the amount of information we can

absorb and use. But, especially when it comes to consumer goods—and consumer advertising constitutes the greater proportion of the propaganda of which the average citizen is aware—we are not getting even a fraction of the information we can use. Millions of dollars are spent on newspaper and magazine ads and on radio and television to tell us that X motor oil contains "additive R-533," and that Y toothpaste contains "Gardol," and that Z cleanser is now colored a "magic yellow," and that M cold tablets give "four-way protection," and that N liver pills are "just like a doctor's prescription." Is this information? Under present conditions, so far as mass communication (propaganda) channels are concerned, the chances of getting information are so slight as to be negligible.

Millions of dollars are spent annually to convince us that having two hundred and seventy-five horsepower in a passenger car contributes to our safety, that a jerry-built shack becomes an "estate" when it's located in "Beverley Acres," and that although you can take up to thirty-six months to pay, there "is no interest or carrying charge." The distrust of propaganda does not come from the fear that someone else is making our choices. It doesn't matter who has influenced our choices if they turn out to be the right ones—indeed, we are grateful to those who give us reliable information, even if it is an advertising agency. The distrust arises from the fact that we are constantly learning (too late) that we have made the wrong choices on the basis of misinformation that someone or other has been at considerable pains and cost to place before us. (The "guaranteed, kiln-dried," 4" x 4" redwood lumber I bought for house remodeling turned out, on sawing, to have a dark, wet core two inches in diameter right through the middle.)

Catton asks, "To what degree do propaganda analysts (including some general semanticists and sociologists) foster this public distrust of socially indispensable communication channels?" I would say in reply that insofar as communication is "socially indispensable," it will inculcate the opposite of "signal reactions," as I understand this term. That does not mean that there will be any dissolution of cultural patterns, but, rather, it will mean the strengthening of society. A sane society will be held together not by incantation or magic words, but by meaningful communication—*i.e.*, communication in which there is an observable correspondence between verbal map and nonverbal territory. Under such conditions, reasoned faith and routine choices can freely exist. One will be able to say of an advertised product or a political party, "Its performance in the past has corresponded with its claims. Hence I have reason to believe that I can put my trust in it again." The social order has nothing to fear from the general semanticist, the propaganda analyst, or any other such disinterested critic of existing communications. If the social order is menaced, it is by the flood of sheer claptrap that so dominates commercial communication channels that thereby all communications are made suspect.

The dissemination of such information and evaluations as will insure the continued functioning of our society as a society must be performed *responsibly*. Catton rightly says that the "epidemic of propaganditis results less from an abundance of misleading propaganda claims than from a shortage of unbiased yet understandable word-maps of human valuing." But has he paid sufficient attention to the fact that the abundance of the one is indissolubly connected with the shortage of the other?

The dissemination of "simple and misleading word-maps" as to the advantages, for example, of a brand of toothpaste commands the talent resources of artists, writers, musicians, comedians, news commentators, dramatists, and the technical resources of a vast, nationwide communications industry, all of which talents unite to attract an audience to the message, sweeten it, and place it in every home.

An *unbiased* word-map on the same subject, however, can get into Consumers Union *Reports* or the *Journal* of the American Dental Association—but where else? Even the school-room channels of communication are systematically infiltrated by prepared "educational materials" (concerning canned goods, oil products, et cetera) thoughtfully provided by industry sources. There is no evidence that the public prefers "simple and misleading word-maps" to other kinds or to no maps at all. The public is given no choice in the matter.

Catton suggests a research project of "concerted efforts toward the careful, objective mapping of human evaluative behavior," as a result of which might arise the "invention and inauguration of some institutional pattern of society which can insure that those who disseminate propaganda on a large scale are agents of the whole community and not merely autonomous opportunists." Why does he ignore the institutional patterns of this kind that already exist—on a national scale in almost all civilized countries and on smaller scales within our own country? I refer, of course, to such institutions as the British Broadcasting Corporation, the Canadian Broadcasting Corporation, Radiodiffusion Française, Japan Radio, and such local institutions in the U.S. as the Wisconsin State Network and the new nonprofit educational television stations that are being developed in most American cities. There are many forms of such publicly responsible institutions; none of them is perfect, but their performance and effectiveness as "agents of the whole community" are matters of public record, open for examination by anyone.

The tragedy of communication by radio and television in the U.S. is that such "agents of the whole community" must exist on a tiny scale where they exist at all. A publicly supported educational television station ordinarily operates on an annual budget of less than is spent for a single commercial network "spectacular." The Wisconsin legislature a few years ago threw out a proposal for a publicly supported television network in that state. Stations that are "agents of the whole community" in U.S. radio and television usually lead a humble and financially precarious existence, some of them broadcasting only a few hours a day, and often ignored in the program listings of the newspapers. And no one even suggests a federal, government-sponsored, nationwide network.

Why do we in the U.S. fear to have that which all other nations find essential? Why, when even so conservative a mind as Herbert Hoover declared in 1924 that an instrument of communication as important as radio should never be commercially exploited, did we virtually turn over the entire miracle of electronic communication to the hucksters, the hawkers, and the pitchmen?

One important reason for this incredible giveaway, I am sure, is the fact that the public has been well propagandized into a signal reaction that identifies government control of anything with "creeping socialism," "tyranny," "communism," or some such abstraction suggesting the dimunution of our liberties. To quote Bernays again, "Those who manipulate this unseen mechanism of society [propaganda] constitute an invisible government which is the true ruling power of our country." Fleeing the imagined tyranny of a visible government, we have delivered ourselves into the hands of this invisible government. Without a powerful and rival channel of communication to speak as "agents of the whole community," there is no alternative to being thus manipulated and invisibly (and therefore irresponsibly) ruled.

To be sure, radio and television stations are licensed to operate "in the public interest," and they occasionally make token gestures in that direction. But will they ever become *disinterested* channels of communication? I don't see how, given the present economics of the industry. And as long as there exists a near-monopoly of our most pervasive and powerful channels of communication, we shall remain Whittaker'd, Baxter'd, and bewildered.

A sharp distinction must be maintained between those uniformities of reaction which result in inappropriate or self-defeating behavior ("signal reactions") and those uniformities of reaction which, whether for reasons of economy and efficiency or for reasons of social cohesion, are necessary to daily living. I would call efforts to induce the former kind of uniformity "propaganda"—in a pejorative sense—whether conducted by advertising agencies or schools. I would call efforts to produce the latter kind of uniformity—again whether conducted by advertising agencies or schools—a necessary part of public education.

IX

CHANGE AND PERMANENCE

THE backgrounds of semantics, the original purpose of
which was the clarification of meanings, were in science.
If I may make a complicated story as simple as possible,
two, and only two, kinds of statements were, in the early
stages of semantics, acknowledged to be meaningful. The first
is the naming statement, such as "Mehitabel and Tober-
mory are cats" and "A bachelor is an unmarried man." ("Unmarried men may also be called bachelors.") Statements of
this kind are about language, in that they instruct us what
names to use for what situations, or as equivalents for other
words.

The second kind of statement acknowledged to be meaningful is the pointing statement—one that describes any kind
of situation that may be pointed to: "The car is in the garage." Such a statement stands for a state of affairs in the ob-

servable world, and we may, if we wish, go out to the garage to see if the statement is or is not true. Statements of scientific fact, as well as all other purportedly factual statements, belong in this category. They are statements that have, in the language of semantics, "referents" in external reality.

The early semanticists (including the so-called "logical positivists") threw all remaining kinds of statements—metaphysical statements, lyrical poetry, value judgments, hortative utterances, and no doubt most of law and jurisprudence—into a vast kitchen midden generously labeled "emotive utterances" (Ogden and Richards), "pseudo-propositions" (the logical positivists), or, less technically, "nonsense."

There was a reason for this dogmatism and ruthlessness. The early semanticists—especially the logical positivists— were interested strictly in cleaning up the language of science, in which nonreferential terms mistakenly assumed to be referential can (and do) cause needless confusion. As Rudolf Carnap writes in *Philosophy and Logical Syntax*: "Thus we find a great similarity between metaphysics and lyrics. But there is one decisive difference between them. Both have no representative function, no theoretical content. A metaphysical proposition, however—as, distinguished from a lyrical verse—seems to have some, and by this not only is the reader deceived, but the metaphysician himself. . . . The danger lies in the deceptive character of metaphysics; it gives the illusion of knowledge without actually giving any knowledge."

In thus laying down the conditions of meaningfulness in scientific discourse, the logical positivists introduced needed rigor into scientific thought. But they did not worry about the special kinds of meaning in, for example, poetic statements. Nor did they concern themselves with ethical statements or the language of law. These problems they left, if they thought about them at all, for others to deal with.

If the meaning of naming statements ("analytic propositions") resides in the rules of language, and if the meaning of pointing statements ("synthetic propositions") resides in the external world, the meaning of "emotive utterances" or "pseudo-propositions" can be said to lie in the nervous system of the speaker or hearer. This is obviously so in the case of a simple "lyrical" statement such as "Ouch!"—which simply expresses an internal condition. It is equally so in the somewhat more complex statement "Life is essentially tragic," even if the theme is elaborated through a volume or two of philosophizing. But such "lyrical" utterances by no means constitute the entire class of statements whose meanings can be said to lie in the nervous system of the speaker. The threefold classification of uses of language into naming statements, pointing statements, and emotive statements—with the implication that emotive statements are not capable of being seriously discussed—omits much that a serious student of meaning must take into consideration. For our present purposes, the most important omission is a consideration of the language of social agreement.

At some time around the age of three or four, children learn to react meaningfully to expressions such as "It's my turn"; "It's Billy's turn next." "My turn" is something that cannot be pointed to—its meaning is not "referential" in the strictly positivist sense—nor is it merely "lyrical." Nevertheless, the meaning of the expression does lie within the nervous systems of the speaker and hearer. It is an elementary form of social agreement. It says something about both the present and the future. With the achievement of the child's ability to react meaningfully to "my turn" and "Billy's turn," there is rejoicing in the heart of his parent or play-school teacher—for the child has taken a significant step toward being socialized—which is to say, human.

Also, at these early stages of life, the child learns to react acceptably to such expressions as "naughty," "good manners," "bad manners," "not fair," and so on. These are, of course, judgmental statements, the meanings of which are in the nervous system of the parent who utters them—"I approve (disapprove) of what you are doing." At first the child simply obeys—he has to. But sooner or later he begins (as the parent says) to "understand"—which means that the child begins to share the parent's approval and disapproval of given courses of action. The parent's judgments have been, as they say in psychoanalysis, "introjected"—that is, the meaning of such terms as "naughty" is now in the nervous system of the child as well as that of the parent. Most of the bringing up of children (to say nothing of the process of "making good citizens") is the process of getting the young to hold such value judgments in common with their elders. These commonly held value judgments are another form of social agreement.

The language of law is the most formidable and most formalized portion of that larger collection of linguistic events that we have termed the language of social agreement. But in the very act of saying "language of social agreement," it appears to me that we distort the facts, since without the language there could not be the kind of social agreement that exists at the human level. The difference between use and ownership, between cohabitation and marriage, between a killing and a murder, is a linguistic product. "Cohabitation" says something about the present, and perhaps, too, about the past; but it makes no commitments about the future. The very fact that commitments can be made rests upon our ability to talk—our ability to make abstractions and symbolizations about the future. "Sirloin next Sunday" is meaningless to a dog, since to a dog a sign has no significance unless its referent is present or immediately forthcoming. But human beings formulate goals for "next Sunday," for "thirty days after date," "until death do us part," or for even longer periods—thereby imposing some kind of order and predictability upon behavior. Social agreements, which are commitments about the future, statements of intent, are made in language—or they are not made at all. As Aldous Huxley writes in *Words and Their Meaning*:

"The existence of language permits human beings to behave with a degree of purposefulness, perseverance and consistency unknown among the other mammals and comparable only to the purposefulness, perseverance and consistency of insects acting under the compulsive force of instinct. Every instant in the life, say, of a cat or a monkey tends to be irrelevant to every other instant. Such creatures are the victims of their moods. Each impulse as it makes itself felt carries the animal away completely. Thus, the urge to fight will suddenly be interrupted by the urge to eat; the all absorbing passion of love will be displaced in the twinkling of an eye by a no less absorbing passion to search for fleas. The consistency of human behaviour, such as it is, is due entirely to the fact that men have formulated their desires, and subsequently rationalized them, in terms of words. . . . If it were not for the descriptive and justificatory words with which we bind our days together, we should live like the animals in a series of discrete and separate spurts of impulse."

Law is the mighty collective effort made by human beings to inhibit the "discrete and separate spurts of impulse" and to organize in their place that degree of order, uniformity, and predictability of behavior that makes society possible.

There is a tremendous difference, therefore, between the "predictability" of science and that of law. What science predicts ("Ice will melt at temperatures above 32° F.") comes true independent of our volition. What law predicts ("Persons convicted of murder will be hanged") comes true because we are resolved to do what we said we would do. At the basis of law is our own resolve—our "agreement," our "willingness," our "intent."

Among the many things we do with words and symbols is to organize not only our past experiences and present perceptions, but also our future behavior. Language is not only descriptive, in the sense of supplying verbal "maps" of nonverbal "territories." It is also prescriptive or directive in the sense of supplying us with verbal "blueprints" of nonverbal "territories" which we intend, through our own efforts, to bring into being. The language of law is of necessity, therefore, to a large degree hortatory. In addition to prescribing certain forms of behavior, it must also create the intent, the resolve, to follow the prescription. The judge is to a large degree a preacher. The trial is to a large degree a morality play.

Hortatory utterances are almost invariably stated at a higher level of abstraction and with a greater degree of dogmatism than the immediate situation calls for. The reasons for this are partly rhetorical: to get attention and to impress the directive firmly on the hearer's mind. The rhetoric in turn is dictated by the human need, in both the speaker and the hearer, for apparent "purposefulness, perseverance, and consistency" in human behavior.

To reduce this matter to a simple example, let us suppose that the purpose of a given hortative utterance is to get Junior to eat his peas. If the simple demand "Junior, eat your peas" does not work, one proceeds immediately to a higher level of abstraction: "Vegetables are good for you," and "All growing boys should get plenty of vegetables." In other words, my demand that Junior eat his peas is asserted to be not merely a passing whim, but the particularization of a general nutritive principle. If Junior still leaves his peas untouched, one appeals to history: "Your grandfather was a vegetarian, and he lived to the age of ninety-nine," and "Sailors in the old sailing ships used to die of scurvy because they didn't get enough fresh vegetables." From here on, it is but a short jump to say that God intended that peas be eaten and that fathers be obeyed.

But the great principles we enunciate on one day prove to be extremely inconvenient on another day, as inevitably they must, since they stated so much more than was necessary to begin with. So, as father himself leaves untouched the carrot-and-raisin salad a few days later, he can say, if challenged, "What I was arguing for all along is not vegetables as such, but for a balanced diet—and it is possible to achieve balance without this particular salad. A man can't keep going on rabbit food. Did you know that Vilhjalmur Stefansson proved that one can live healthily and well on an all-meat diet? Do you know of the millions in Asia who are suffering from protein deficiency because they get nothing but vegetables to eat?" Thus do fathers keep all bases covered and strive to maintain the fiction of infallible wisdom.

If the layman regards the law with a mixture of exaggerated respect and exaggerated distrust, is it not because lawyers and judges perform in a spectacular and awe-inspiring way what the rest of us do daily? Judges, when they change the interpretation of the Constitution, are almost always at considerable pains to assert that their new interpretation is what the Constitution really meant all along. If we, as laymen, approve of the change, we agree that this is indeed what the Constitution meant all along. If we disapprove the change, we are furious at the temerity of judges who take it upon themselves to "change the Constitution."

The hortatory habit of mind, if too uncritically indulged, whether by laymen or by jurists, results in a proclivity for claiming for one's exhortations a longer-lasting validity and a wider generality of applicability than any immediate situation would warrant.

Such remarks as "The law is what the judge says it is"

and Mr. Dooley's "No matter whether th' constitution follows th' flag or not, th' Supreme Coort follows th' iliction returns" are usually made with sarcastic or cynical intent. This so because it is widely assumed—by lawyers as well as by laymen —that "the law" is, or should be, something eternal and changeless, which undergoes attrition only because judges and legislatures, like other men, are afflicted with something called "human nature." When it is pointed out that laws do change with every session of the legislature, the reply is usually to the effect that of course minor adjustments in particular statutes and regulations are constantly being made, but that the "principles" remain unchanged. It is this assumption of a transcendental, changeless "law" that was mockingly described by Justice Holmes as "a brooding omnipresence in the sky."

The belief, implicit or explicit, in such a brooding omnipresence is an almost inevitable product, it appears to me, of the hortatory habit of mind, which involves, as I have argued, frequent recourse to extremely high levels of abstraction. Impelled simultaneously by a need to give generality to one's directives and a need to be consistent, we dream up a heaven of abstract principles—principles that are thought of as dwelling together in perfect and harmonious logical order. This heavenly order gives moral sanction to the earthly, practical decisions arrived at. Jerome Frank, in *Law and the Modern Mind,* gives the following description of such a transcendental system:

"And this Bealish Law can approximate perfection. It can have, to use Beale's phrase, 'purity of doctrine,' free from 'warping by bad precedent.' It can be rid of disturbing novelties and aberrations. It can be a harmonious closed system of principles, not marred by discontinuities, a system from which correct rules can be infallibly and unhesitatingly worked out. In this realm of pure Law, the answer to a particular problem can always be correct. In the sub-lunar world in which the courts dwell, mistakes will happen. But such mistakes are not Law. For such apparent law is not real. Mistaken law is not 'truly law,' even if the courts stubbornly act as if it were.

"In short, real law, for Beale, is superhuman."

However, Thurman Arnold, in his brilliant and amusing work *The Symbols of Government,* states that an examination of this supposedly harmonious system, as enunciated in the literature of jurisprudence, reveals neither harmony nor system, but merely a restatement in a more difficult and abstract vocabulary of the contradictions and bewilderments of daily living. The jurists and scholars who devote themselves to the contemplation of this supposed divine order Arnold characterizes as "priestly-minded men."

Being myself a member of a profession (a teacher of English) that is to a large degree hortatory in its functions, I repeatedly find in my colleagues both the tendencies described, although I should hasten to add that I do not find them as often today as I used to. First, there is the idea of "good English," toward which it is the duty of the English teacher constantly to goad his pupils. This results in the creation of a heavenly never-never land of people who speak nothing but "good English." To justify the nagging of pupils and the red-penciling of their written themes, all sorts of abstract grammatical and rhetorical principles are appealed to. These principles often contradict each other and are habitually ignored by working writers, speakers, and journalists —especially the most effective ones; nevertheless, they are believed to have a profoundly salutary effect. (It is difficult to imagine a linguistic principle to justify the correct reading of the sentence "There was a tear in his shirt and a tear in his eye," although teachers make constant appeals to consistency. Furthermore, nobody ever takes the double negative of "I ain't got no money" to mean the affirmative "I have money," but the reason still given for avoiding the double negative is that it constitutes an affirmative.)

Concerned with improvement and uplift, and therefore with the celestial mechanics of the legal heavens, the "priestly-minded man," according to Arnold, tends to ignore as inconsequential and irrelevant much that happens on earth —in magistrates' courts and other such unscholarly places, because, with his habits of mind, he "cannot look at the world as it is without a shudder." The reader will no doubt recall from his own secondary-school experience the teacher of English to whom a like description might have been applied: concerned with the improvement and uplift of student English and therefore with the grammatical terminology and rules of an unrealistically defined "good English," the priestly-minded English teacher was the poorest kind of observer of the actualities of language, because she (it was often a she) could not listen to American English as it is spoken without a shudder. Such English teachers, instead of taking notes (as H. L. Mencken did) on what was happening, simply cringed at the way the English language was daily being "abused."

The differences among the regional and class dialects of the United States, the actualities of usage and vocabulary-development among farmers, auto workers, disk jockeys, radiation-laboratory technicians, jazz musicians, and newspaper columnists—these were not and in some places still are not considered fit objects of study in departments of English composition, although nine tenths of the practical communication of the nation is negotiated through just such dialects. The high priests of linguistic etiquette never did bother to answer Mark Twain's famous question (or was it Clarence Darrow's?): "When you learn good English, who are you going to talk it to?" Until the fairly recent emergence of a descriptive linguistic science and a descriptive American grammar, the priestly-minded English teachers had the field pretty much to themselves.

In the terminology of the general semantics of Korzybski, the attitude described by Arnold as "priestly-mindedness," and what I have called the "hortatory habit of mind," are both instances of "intensional orientation." Intensional orientation is the habit of orienting oneself by means of words, to the more or less complete exclusion of a consideration of what the words stand for. It is orientation in terms of definitions, prescriptions, categories, Aristotelian "essences." In the apt phrase of Wendell Johnson, it is "letting your language do your thinking for you."

What Korzybski calls the "extensional orientation" is, in contrast, the habit of orienting oneself in terms of the nonverbal realities for which words presumably stand, to which words are often an imperfect guide, and from which we are too often shielded by verbal smoke screens. It is an orientation of fact-mindedness, as opposed to word-mindedness. Korzybski proposed his general semantics as a discipline in extensional orientation. His emphasis was on education and mental hygiene, but he regarded his "epistemological re-education" as a generalization of tendencies common to all creative modern thought, in the social as well as physical sciences, in intellectual life no less than in the problems of daily living.

These common tendencies and their parallels in the "functional approach" of the "legal realists" (or, if you will, the "legal positivists"—their intellectual genealogy goes back at least to Jeremy Bentham) have been succinctly described by Felix S. Cohen, in "Transcendental Nonsense and the Functional Approach" (*Columbia Law Review*) :

"In physics, the functional or operational method is an assault upon such supernatural concepts as absolute space and absolute time. . . . Modern 'functional grammar' is an assault upon grammatical theories and distinctions which, as applied to the English language, simply have no verifiable significance. . . . And passing to the field of art, we find that functional architecture is likewise a repudiation of outworn symbols and functionless forms that have no meaning—hollow marble pillars that do not support, fake buttresses, and false fronts.

"So, too, in law. Our legal system is filled with supernatural concepts, that is to say, concepts which cannot be defined in terms of experience, and from which all sorts of empirical decisions are supposed to flow. Against these unverifiable concepts modern jurisprudence presents an ultimatum. Any word that cannot pay up in the currency of fact, upon demand, is to be declared bankrupt, and we are to have no more dealings with it."

This opposition to verbalism unchecked by fact or experience is by no means the only respect in which the "semantics movement," from Ogden and Richards' "finding the referent," to P. W. Bridgman's "operationalism," to Korzybski's "extensional orientation," parallels the thinking of the functionalist school of law. A few other respects in which semantics and legal functionalism run parallel to and reinforce each other may be enumerated. In both there is the determination to eliminate metaphysics. In both there is a sharp awareness of the difference between questions of fact and questions of language, and therefore a determination not to fall into linguistic traps. In both there is awareness of the processes of abstraction and symbolization by means of which human beings organize their perceptions and their knowledge. Consequently, in both there is profound awareness of the deceptive character of any set of abstractions considered apart from the complex of events from which the abstractions were made. In this respect, Thurman Arnold's derisive remarks about our failure to understand society because we persist in studying it in separate compartments called "law," "economics," "sociology," "political science," and so on, fit in exactly with Korzybski's insistence upon the study of man as an "organism-as-a-whole-in-an-environment," and his insistence upon the study of human events in their full biological, ecological, psychological, economic, political, and cultural complexity.

But perhaps the most important respect in which the semanticists and the legal functionalists see eye to eye is their acceptance of the world-as-process, and therefore of society-as-process. According to, for example, the grammatical fundamentalists, to accept the fact of change in grammar and usage is to condone, if not to invite, linguistic anarchy. According to legal fundamentalists, admission of the possibility of change in "the law" is regarded as equally threatening to the social order. The semanticist, the functional grammarian, and the legal functionalist appear to be alike in their rejection of absolutes, and in their confidence that permanence and change can be reconciled in a dynamic concept of order.

What is central to the views of order held by the legal fundamentalists and the functionalists is that they arise from contrasting sets of assumptions about language-fact relationships. Of the former, Jerome Frank writes:

"Legal Absolutism, then, is word-worship? A suggestive hypothesis. Particularly so when we compare the legal Absolutists with another group of persons to whom the abstract term is well-nigh divine—the metaphysical reasoners of whom Plato is the arch-type. Plato saw that beautiful things become corrupted or die, that men who seem noble in character do evil deeds. The evanescence of values was painful to him. How make them permanent? Plato found an ingenious answer: The 'Beautiful' endures even when beautiful roses wither or beautiful youths become old and ugly. The 'Good' remains good when good men grow wicked. Such terms are the names of imperishable entities. . . . These universals are stable; they are therefore the Real. Thus Plato found relief from unbearable chance and change in the stable meaning of words; thus, by fooling himself with words, he reached 'the region of purity, eternity, immortality and unchangeableness' at which he aimed, finding it only in the most abstract. 'Abstraction was the Jacob's ladder by which the philosopher ascended to certainty. The further he was from the facts, the nearer he thought himself to be to the truth.' "

In contrast to such a Platonic view is that held by such a modern British scholar as Glanville Williams, who writes in the *Law Quarterly Review*:

"The view of the semanticist may perhaps be stated as follows. All universals are arrived at by a process of abstraction. . . . Abstraction may be defined as the imaginative selection of some one characteristic of a complex situation so that it may be attended to in isolation. . . . Abstraction is, in short, the perception of similarity in spite of differences.

"The importance of abstraction in our thinking cannot be stressed too much. 'Without abstraction there can be no recognition of similarity; without the recognition of similarity there can be no advance in knowledge' (Stebbings). But the process has its dangers. The danger is particularly present when we objectify ('hypostatize') our abstractions. As a matter of linguistic convenience we are accustomed to hypostatize words expressing qualities or properties, thus speaking of (say) 'justice' or 'redness' as though these things were part of the stuff of nature. But semantically there is no difference between the adjectives 'just' and 'red' and the nouns 'justice' and 'redness'; the difference is only in grammatical form. Qualities like these are not to be found by themselves anywhere. . . . To speak of redness apart from red things is like speaking of the grin without the Cheshire cat."

If, then, language is a set of abstractions, constructed according to the conventions of one's tongue and modified according to changing events and changing needs, the fact of change in the meanings and interpretations of words, from context to context and over the course of time, need not be contemplated with a shudder. Change is simply a fact. Novelty is also a fact. And the inability of human beings to agree on the applicability of old abstractions to new situations is neither to be wondered at nor deplored. In a way, what human beings are constantly trying to do is to describe the Battle of Britain in Anglo-Saxon—which means that the battle is distorted because of the shortcomings of language, or that the language is stretched and distorted and given novel meanings because of the demands of the event. As Williams further writes:

"I have already pointed a number of legal morals in the course of this section [on types of uncertainty in legal terminology], but some general conclusions of legal interest remain to be drawn.

"(1) In the first place, the theory here advanced destroys completely and forever the illusion that the law can be completely certain. Since the law has to be expressed in words, and words have a penumbra of uncertainty, marginal cases are bound to occur. Certainty in law is thus seen to be a matter of degree. (2) Correlatively, the theory destroys the illusion that the function of the judge is simply to administer the law. If marginal cases must occur, the function of the judge in adjudicating upon them must be legislative. The distinction between the mechanical administration of fixed rules and free judicial discretion is thus a matter of degree, not the sharp distinction that it is sometimes assumed to be."

Among present-day teachers of English—at least those who have been trained in modern linguistic science—it is believed that accurate knowledge of the facts of current usage in different social classes, on different social occasions, among different occupational groups, and in different areas of the country, and knowledge of the processes of linguistic change are essential if one is to develop in his students the ability to write and speak well. The emphasis in instruction is not upon authoritarian rules and principles, but upon the development of curiosity and habits of accurate observation of language-in-process, whether in the writings of Dickens, at chamber of commerce meetings, or in labor-organizing drives. Styles of discourse, whether in scientific papers or in underworld argot, are studied, and their effectiveness within their social context is noted. Such training in linguistic observation produces students who, instead of being petrified into inarticulateness by stilted notions of "correctness," take delight in the variety and richness of the English language, and seek to cultivate that flexibility of linguistic resources that will enable them to take in stride whatever problems of communication they may encounter.

Just as functional grammarians try to understand how language works, the legal functionalists, if I understand them rightly, try to understand how society works, not through knowledge of law alone, but through acquaintance with the workings of the commercial, industrial, educational, military, political, and other institutions out of whose activities and interplay arise the problems that lawyers must deal with. Competent in the law, yet trained to observe without prejudice what is going on in a changing society, the legal functionalist would make of the law not a body of shibboleths, not an entangling web of verbal taboos, but an increasingly efficient instrument for the orderly negotiation of day-to-day adjustments and accommodations in the relations of individuals and institutions to each other. The sum of these accommodations, made in such a way as to leave in their wake a minimum of dissatisfaction, prevents the building up of those pressures that make orderly change impossible, and creates that combination of stability and flexibility that characterizes every viable society.

In modern mathematics there is a phrase, "invariance under transformation," which I have found increasingly meaningful as I consider the problems of lawyers, English teachers, and all of us in a period of bewildering change. If you draw a figure of intersecting lines and curves on a rubber sheet, then stretch or distort the sheet in different directions, the lengths of the lines will change, the angles at which they meet each other will change, the sizes of enclosed areas will change, but certain relationships among the lines will remain "invariant" despite the many "transformations." The abstracting of what is invariant through many transformations is, then, as in the mathematical field of topology from which the foregoing example is drawn, the description of what remains constant in spite of apparently drastic changes, the description of the elements of permanence in apparent impermanence.

What characterizes the semanticist and the legal functionalist, then, as well as others in the forefront of contemporary thought, is the ability to come to terms with change and impermanence, in the knowledge that what seems at one level of abstraction to be change may be at another level of abstraction but another instance of the same thing. To come to terms with the world-as-process is also to come to terms with society-as-process. And to come to terms with society-as-process instead of retiring in confusion or trying to escape from change into a never-never land of Eternal Verities, is to be able to function effectively, whether as lawyer, English teacher, or citizen, and also to be able to direct those changes somewhat closer to the heart's desire.

LANGUAGE, CULTURE, AND ART

MOST people assume that language is the "expression of thought." Such a statement contains the unspoken implication that we first have a "thought," and then "express" it by "putting it into words." Benjamin Lee Whorf, along with such scholars as Edward Sapir and Leonard Bloomfield, established the fact that thought and language are *not* such independent processes as traditional accounts imply. Indeed, these modern students of language reversed, for all practical purposes, the traditional notion that a thought comes first, to be followed later by a linguistic formulation of the thought. As Whorf, who was an authority on Mayan and Aztec and American Indian languages, put it: "We dissect nature along lines laid down by our native languages. The categories and types that we isolate from the world of phenomena we do not find there because they stare every observer in the face; on the contrary, the world is presented in a kaleidoscopic flux of impressions which has to be organized by our minds—and this means largely by the linguistic systems in our minds. We cut nature up, organize it into concepts, and ascribe significances as we do, largely because we are parties to an agreement to organize it in this way—an agreement that holds throughout our speech community and is codified in the patterns of language. The agreement is, of course, an implicit and unstated one, *but its terms are absolutely obligatory;* we cannot talk at all except by subscribing to the organization and classification of data which the agreement decrees." Or, if I may state it more briefly if a little less exactly, what Whorf means is that the kind of language we speak largely determines the kind of thoughts we have; we cannot speak without imposing upon the flux of experience an assumed structure implied by the formal or grammatical structure of the language we happen to speak.

Let me illustrate with one of Whorf's own examples. He contrasts the English language and that of the Shawnee Indians in their ways of isolating or abstracting different data from experience to describe a given situation. The English sentence "I clean the gun with a ramrod" has, in addition to the words "I" and "gun," three items isolated from experience: "clean," "with," and "ramrod." In describing this situation in Shawnee, expressions for "I" and "gun" are present, but the rest of the statement is made by three isolates or abstractions not present in the English language, namely, "dry space," "interior of hole," and "motion of instrument," so that presumably the Shawnee sentence would become, if it had to be given anything like a literal translation, "I/dry space/interior of hole/motion of instrument/the gun."

Perhaps a couple of further examples will make clearer this principle of the structures created by language. In English, in order to make a sentence at all we have to use at least one each of two classes of words, namely, nouns and verbs—

one to denote the actor and the other the action, as in "The boy runs," "The frog jumps." The limitation of this structure is revealed most clearly in those cases where the actor and action are inseparable, as in such sentences as "It rains," "It snows," where a purely syntactical actor, "it," is supplied for the purpose of meeting the structural requirements of an English sentence. As Whorf further says in the same essay: "In the Hopi language, lightning, wave, flame, meteor, puff of smoke, pulsation, are verbs—events of necessarily brief duration cannot be anything but verbs. Cloud and storm are at about the lower limit of duration for nouns. Hopi, you see, actually has a classification of events (or linguistic isolates) by duration type, something strange to our modes of thought. On the other hand, in Nootka, a language of Vancouver Island, all words seem to us to be verbs . . . we have, as it were, a monistic view of nature that gives us only one class of words for all kinds of events. 'A house occurs' or 'it houses' is the way of saying 'house,' exactly like 'a flame occurs' or 'it burns.' These terms seem to us like verbs because they are inflected for durational and temporal nuances, so that the suffixes of the word for house event make it mean long-lasting house, temporary house, future house, house that used to be, what started out to be a house, and so on."

What is important about facts such as these? From the point of view of anyone interested in the operation of the human mind, the important fact is that any statement or observation of reality is an abstraction—an abstraction dictated by the conventions of one's culture. Where the English-speaking person abstracts from the nameless, subverbal situation the idea of "cleaning with a ramrod," the speaker of Shawnee abstracts the "drying action with a moving instrument on the interior of a hole." The speaker of Shawnee, no less than the speaker of English, feels that his way of describing the situation is the simplest, most obvious, and most natural way of saying it. Until they get together to make systematic comparisons of the kinds of abstractions they make, it will occur to neither speaker that there can be any other way of describing the objective situation than that to which each is accustomed. I have dwelt on this example at some length in order to make clear a fundamental general point, namely, that all languages impose a conventional and more or less arbitrary structure upon the events described. That structure, as Whorf has said, is not given by nature; it does not "stare us in the face," although we may imagine that it does; it is created by the structure of the language we happen to speak.

With this background let us approach the problem of modern art. Just as most people in most cultures tend to regard their words as direct representations of fact, so have we all tended to believe that the traditional and familiar art styles of the West are direct representations (or imitations) of reality. Both in language and in art we have remained largely unconscious of the fact that what we represent through our verbal or visual symbols is not reality itself, but *our abstractions from reality*. But human beings in different cultures and in different epochs abstract and structuralize their experiences in widely different ways—and each way of abstracting makes sense to those who are accustomed to abstracting in that way, while it may make little or no sense to those with other ways of abstracting.

Any period of rapid growth and change, such as the world had been experiencing since the Industrial Revolution, obviously necessitates changes in the ways of abstracting. As A. N. Whitehead has said, "A civilization which cannot burst through its current abstractions is doomed to sterility after a very limited period of progress." A basic general way in which the art revolution of the twentieth century (which had, of course, already begun in the nineteenth century) can be described is to say that artists, sensing perhaps more clearly

than any others save scientists the bankruptcy of the traditional abstractions with which we had been trained to
visualize the world and think about it, started systematically
and even explosively to look for alternative ways of abstracting. This I believe to be the fundamental meaning of the modern movement in art: pointillism, futurism, cubism, surreal-
ism, dadaism, expressionism, fauvism, the interest in Japanese
prints, in Chinese calligraphy, in Italian primitives, in
Oceanic, African, and American Indian art. And it appears to
me more than coincidental that those modern artists who were
philosophically, epistemologically, and semantically most
aware of what they were doing (for example, some of the
theorists of the Bauhaus tradition) have consistently used
such terms as "visual syntax," "grammar of form," and
"language of vision," in describing what they were up to. Modern artists have been, both consciously and unconsciously,
seeking ways of abstracting different from those traditional in
Western culture since the Renaissance. They have been doing
so largely because they are convinced that traditional ways of
seeing are not adequate to express the visual experience of
twentieth-century man and are searching for better ways of
symbolizing our new kind of visual experience. They have
also been doing so simply to explore the many and varied ways
in which we can abstract and organize our abstractions, often,
I suspect, in the way that mathematicians invent new mathematical systems, not for any immediate practical use, but for
the purpose of exploring possibilities.

(I am not saying that modern art, or any part of it,
is "mathematical"—whatever that may mean. I am saying
that some modern artists, especially the abstract, and some
modern mathematicians are engaged in analogous pursuits in
that they both appear interested in creating and exploring the
possibilities of novel symbol-systems. The symbol-systems of
mathematics and of art are entirely different from each

other; hence I do not know what people mean when they say of some abstract artists that their work is "mathematical." Mathematics hasn't a thing to do with the paintings of, for example, Mondrian.)

Modern artists have also—and in this the analogy to linguistic analysis becomes most clear—dissected the materials of their language for us. By this I mean that when we look at a traditional painting, we are made to think as little as possible of the canvas, the brush strokes, the paint, and the wood; we are made to think about the object painted—the woman, the tree, the mountain, or whatever. Modern artists, on the contrary, have encouraged us to examine the materials out of which their languages are put together, as if they were saying to us, "Look, this is paint; this is wood; this is a piece of rope; this is corrugated paper—and this is what can be said with these materials!"

Breaking down the materials of their art languages, exploring the possibilities of the picture surface, trying out new kinds of perspective or avoiding it altogether, attempting to convey the new spatial experiences of the twentieth century, scientifically analyzing the psychological facts about the minute tensions produced in the eye by the experiences of color and color combination, the modern artist has been and still is engaged in the process of evolving the new visual languages more adequate to the feel of twentieth-century experience than the art languages of the immediate European and American past.

Hence, "modern art" is not one tendency, but a collection of many—some, like Mondrian, in the direction of the purely abstract; some, like Klee and Chagall, in the direction of the fanciful manipulation of known symbols which are given new dimensions of meaning; some, like Leger, deeply interested in the impact of the machine on modern sensibility; some, like Duchamp and Calder, interested in introducing the time dimension into art to make the art object an experience of motion; some, like Braque in his collages, insisting that paper be seen as paper, canvas as canvas, paint as paint; some, like Dali and other surrealists, interested in producing the maximum optical illusions of depth, roundness of form, moisture, and texture. In spite of these wide divergencies of style and aim, however, we lump these many tendencies together to call them all "modern," and it is worth noting that most people interested in what is called "modern" are interested simultaneously in contradictory and divergent manifestations of artistic modernity.

This fact, too, seems to me to call for explanation. Traditional Western philosophies have almost always believed, after one fashion or another, in Truth with a capital T. It has long been felt, for example, that it is the function of the artist to grasp the "essence" of things, and to reveal the "Truth" and "universal order" underlying the accidents of appearance. Perhaps such a neoclassicist as Alexander Pope expressed as clearly as anybody this belief in a discoverable "universal order":

> All Nature is but art, unknown to thee;
> All chance, direction, which thou canst not see;
> All discord, harmony not understood;
> All partial evil, universal good.

The artist's intuition is supposed, under this theory, to rise above particularities and to arrive at "essences," whereby "Truth" and "Beauty" and "Order" stand revealed. To quote still another neoclassicist, Sir Joshua Reynolds: "The whole beauty and grandeur of the Art [of painting] consists, in my opinion, in being able to get above all singular forms, local customs, particularities, and details of every kind. All the objects which are exhibited to our view by Nature, upon close examination will be found to have blemishes and defects. . . . But it is not every eye that perceives these blemishes. It must be an eye long used to the contemplation and comparison of forms; and which, by a long habit of observing what any set of objects of the same kind have in common, has acquired the power of discerning what each wants in particular. This long laborious comparison should be the first study of the Painter who aims at the greatest style. By this means, he acquires a just idea of beautiful forms; he corrects Nature by herself, her imperfect state by her more perfect. . . . As the idea of beauty is of necessity but one, so there can be but one great mode of painting."

And again: "The natural appetite or taste of the human mind is for Truth; whether that truth results from the real agreement or equality of original ideas among themselves; from the agreement of the representation of any object with the thing represented; or from correspondence of the several parts of any arrangement with each other. It is the very same taste that relishes a demonstration in geometry, that is pleased with the resemblance of a picture to an original, and touched with the harmony of music. All these have unalterable and fixed foundations in nature."

"All these have unalterable and fixed foundations in nature!" There is then but one Beauty for all time and one Truth. The "universal order" has been there since the Creation, and it is there whether the artist discovers it or not.

Such a theory of Truth, Beauty, and Order is, of course, radically at variance with both current artistic theory and current philosophy of science. There is, according to the modern scientific view, no more order to be found in the universe than we put there by ordering our observations and abstractions and generalizations into systems. For example, Newtonian physics is the ordering of an enormous number of observations about the universe, arranged into a coherent system. When that system was found to be deficient in certain fundamental respects, a still more general system, the physics of Einstein, was evolved, which made possible the inclusion of those observations that could not be fitted into the Newtonian system. Similarly, data that cannot be ordered in terms of algebra may be ordered in terms of the differential calculus. Data that cannot be ordered in a two-valued logic are given an order by a probability logic.

In philosophy of science, we are rapidly discovering in innumerable ways that the "order of the universe" is not something given us from outside, but something created by ourselves, by means of ordering and arranging our perception of the world and our symbolic constructs at all levels of abstraction drawn therefrom into more or less coherent systems.

In other words, there is no one Truth with "unalterable and fixed foundations in nature," nor is there only one Beauty, dictating "but one great mode of painting." Every way of abstracting produces its own kind of truth, which, in the hands of one who orders his abstractions well, results in its own kind of beauty. And the order based on Miró's way of abstracting is different from that based on Mark Tobey's way. Each has its validity, and each has its limitations. And it is characteristic of the modern frame of mind and the modern sensibility that all of us who delight in modern art find pleasure and excitement and order in radically different styles at once. It seems to me, therefore, that although a great deal of our pleasure in modern art lies in our admiration of individual ways of abstracting and ordering abstractions shown by the various artists, still another element in our pleasure is the knowledge we derive that all these ways of abstracting have their legitimacy. We are no longer bound by the cultural provincialism that enabled people in the past to select one favored style, Greco-Roman, or Sung Dynasty Chinese, or any other, and say, "This *alone* is art!" Modern art, with its own experiments as well as with its explorations of exotic arts, has widely enriched for all of us the meaning of art; and the trained modern sensibility, largely because of its education in the formal aspects of visual and plastic experience given by modern artists, is able to understand in their own terms multitudes of artistic idioms, such as the African and Oceanic and American Indian, which were incomprehensible to our immediate critical predecessors.

Modern artists are contributing profoundly to the breakup of cultural provincialism—and in this fact lies, I believe, its deepest relatedness to other forms of modern awareness. The cultural anthropologist and the sociologist, studying different and exotic cultures, try to understand each culture in its own terms. The effect of this attempt, as we all know, is the gradual diminution of that provincialism that stands as a wall between one class and another, between one people and another.

In times past, it used to be possible for us in Western culture to say of the Zuñi Indian, the Dobuan, the Arapesh, the Chinese, or the Russians, "They do as they do, they think as they think, because they don't know any better." The rise of cultural anthropology is a response to our perception of the fact that such provincialism of attitude is inadequate for the purposes of social thinking in the modern world. In comparative linguistics, in semantics, in many of the new psychologies, and in the philosophy of science, we see also the attack upon cultural rigidity, and the attempt to understand the variety of ways in which the world can be seen and made intelligible. We are, in all these fields and in many others, in an age of exploration—an exploration of the possibilities of human thought and vision and cultural and psychological reorganization. It is an age of inward exploration more exciting, possibly, than the exploration of new continents. We cannot any more take our integrations tailor-made as they are handed down by any one culture. We are compelled by historic necessity to examine all the possibilities—and, in one way or another, to try to roll our own.

XI

THE UNACKNOWLEDGED LEGISLATORS

"POETS," said Shelley, "are the unacknowledged legislators of the world." This remark has often been shrugged off as a typical romantic overstatement. But I believe that the students of art and design must take it seriously. Ernst Cassirer, in his book *An Essay on Man,* has written, "No longer in a merely physical universe, man lives in a symbolic universe. Language, myth, art, and religion are parts of this universe. . . . No longer can man confront reality immediately; he cannot see it, as it were, face to face. . . . He has so enveloped himself in linguistic forms, in artistic images, in musical symbols or religious rites that he cannot see or know anything except by the interposition of this artificial medium."

Or, to put it in alternative terms, human beings live in a "semantic environment," which is the creation of their symbol systems, so that even the individual who believes himself to be in direct contact with reality, and therefore free of doctrines and assumptions, thinks in terms of the symbols with which he has been taught to organize his perceptions, namely, the visual or verbal symbols, or images, which are the currency with which communication is negotiated in his culture.

The symbol, as Susanne Langer says, is the basic instrument of thought. And those who create new symbols, whether as scientists, poets, novelists, dramatists, artists, or sculptors, are those who, by giving us new instruments to think with, give us new areas to explore in our thinking. And poets and artists are indeed the unacknowledged legislators of the world if, by giving us new symbols, they give all of us, including members of Congress, new areas of insight and sensitivity—a sensitivity ultimately expressed, perhaps fifty, perhaps a hundred years later, in new legislation and new social institutions.

The creation of symbols—the basic tools with which to think and feel—is then the fundamental task of the artist and, as Robert Oppenheimer has suggested, of the genuinely creative theoretical scientist. These are the people who give us our tools to think with.

The symbols of the scientist have their special uses, for theoretical clarification, for system building, for practical application, but what of the symbols of daily living—the verbal and visual symbols in terms of which we negotiate our day-to-day problems? We sort out, organize, and think about the data of our daily experience with two sets of tools: verbal symbols and visual symbols. With our verbal symbols we describe the world, ask questions of ourselves and others, make decisions with the answers. With our visual symbols, by which I mean the images, the image clusters, the visual stereotypes inside our heads, we also sort out and organize and think about the data of our daily experience, and create with them our pictures of the world.

With these systems of symbols inside our heads, we look out upon the world around us, and we find, or we persuade ourselves that we find, correspondences between the pictures inside our heads and the world outside. Believing these correspondences to be real, we feel at home in what we regard as a known world.

But are our symbolic tools adequate? If the symbols, the abstractions, the words, the phrases, the visual images, the interpretative stereotypes that we have inherited from our cultural environment are adequate, we are indeed adjusted to reality. But what if they are not? Like other instruments, languages select, and in selecting what they select, they omit what they do not select. The thermometer, which speaks one kind of language, knows nothing of weight. If temperature matters and weight does not, what the thermometer says is adequate. But if weight or color or odor or factors other than temperature matter, then the language of the thermometer is not adequate. Every language, every system of symbols, leaves work undone for other languages to do.

At the center of the modern movement in art has been the systematic attempt to overthrow the static, object-mindedness of older traditions in art in favor of a dynamic, relation-mindedness. There was, of course, a reason for the emergence into importance of time-and-relation-mindedness for the twentieth-century painter. Vision is a means of orienting ourselves in space. In an age of trains, automobiles, and airplanes, in an age in which the mere task of getting across our city streets alive requires to an unprecedented degree the ability to interpret space-time relationships of moving objects, the old vision became totally inadequate. Modern artists, since as long ago as the Italian futurists, have been compelled by technological necessity to think in space-time relationships of a new kind. The artist, if he is to train our vision and convey adequately the feel of modern visual experience, has to create images in which time is a factor.

Another important facet of the modern movement in art has been the explicit recognition of the symbolic character of art. Rejecting the Aristotelian definition of art as imitation, modern art has tried in a variety of ways to replace the notion of a painting as representation with the idea of a painting as a symbol. And the new ways of symbolizing, and the new assumptions underlying these new ways, have been the subject for the last few decades of heated debate; but by now the point is clearly established that it is no longer the job of the painter to produce likenesses, but to produce symbols—even if we have difficulty often in figuring out just what is being symbolized!

These and other tendencies in modern art have been part of a semantic revolution that has been going on in our times— a revolution in our assumptions about the nature of our knowings. In the old orientation, in the semantics of fixed, known "objects," summarized in the conviction that "pigs is pigs," adjustments to life were made, at higher levels of abstraction, on the basis of fixed definitions and categories: men are men, women are women, government is government, business is business, Europe is Europe, America is America, and so on.

Suddenly, however, the entire system of static evaluations, under the impact of the rapid development of scientific knowledge and technology in the past hundred and fifty years, has been rendered obsolete. With increasing rapidity in our own times, we have seen the old categories crumble, so that objects and entities as such no longer mean very much; today all fields of knowledge are concerned with relations. As Arthur S. Eddington has said with respect to the "physical" sciences, "The relativity theory of physics reduces everything to relations; that is to say, it is structure, not material, that counts." We have been taught by modern science that the so-called "objective world" itself is a relationship between the observer and the observed, so that ultimately we are able to know nothing but that relationship.

Modern art and music, then, like all modern thought, are attempts to overthrow age-old habits of thought, or semantic patterns—the attempt to overthrow object-mindedness in favor of relation-mindedness, to substitute the dynamic for the static in the basic images with which we create our pictures of the world.

Vision and language are the two most important means we have of apprehending reality. How we talk and how we see determine, more than anything else, how successful we are in coping with our environment. The cultural crises of our times, as one almost gets tired of hearing, is the result of trying to continue into our new world the habits of thought inherited from earlier stages of our culture. The change from the old to the new requires, in a sense, learning to see all over again. Because, as Gyorgy Kepes has written, "Vision is not only orientation in physical spheres, but also orientation in human spheres. . . . In each age of human history man was compelled to search for a temporary equilibrium in his conflicts with nature and in his relation with other men, and thus created, through an organization of visual imagery, a symbolic order of his psychological and intellectual experiences. . . . Today, the dynamics of social events, and the new vistas of a mobile, physical world, have compelled us to exchange a static iconography for a dynamic one."

T. E. Hulme, in his essay on modern art, describes the function of art for primitive people: "They live in a world whose lack of order and seeming arbitrariness must inspire them with a certain fear. . . . In art this state of mind results in a desire to create a certain abstract geometrical shape, which, being durable and permanent, shall be a refuge from the flux and impermanence of outside nature. The need which art satisfies here is not delight in the forms of nature . . . but the exact contrary. In the reproduction of natural objects there is an attempt to purify them of their characteristically living qualities in order to make them necessary and immovable."

In other words, in so-called "primitive" art, West African or American Indian or the art of the South Seas, the attempt is to come to terms with a hostile nature by imposing upon natural forms an intellectual, geometrical order. In this way, these arts serve as equipment for living in an environment filled with unknown terrors. Art, said Hulme, "cannot be understood by itself, but must be taken as one element in a general process of adjustment between man and the outside world. The character of that relation determines the character of the art."

How shall the artist of today come to terms with the present environment? How shall he find the images which, like the sculpture of the West Africans, will bring us to terms with the terror and mystery of our environment? Although many segments of the general public have still not caught up with the modern movement in art of the early twentieth century, already new problems are being presented by the world as we know it through science.

Let me repeat, the task of art is to provide us with images that enable us to symbolize adequately, and therefore think about, the profoundest realities of the times. In medieval times religious images symbolized the realities of God, the angels, and the saints. In Renaissance times the prevailing image was that of the human body, symbolizing the ideas of an age of humanism.

Today the world perceived by the senses is only a part of the total reality we deal with. The new worlds and new forces disclosed by science in the past few decades—by electronics, by astrophysics, by microbiology, by photo-elasticity studies, by the study of nucleo-proteins and their role in genetics, by radioactive tracer studies, and by nuclear physics—these realities are not revealed directly to the senses. They are scientific inferences that present us with what P. W. Bridgman called an "explanatory crisis." The amount and the variety of new knowledge available appear almost too much for our hearts and minds to encompass. Nevertheless, we must create an order out of our present bewilderment.

Creating order which will enable us to come to terms with our new scientific knowledge is a task that confronts us on more than one level. There is the level of the philosopher of science, who will seek to discover in the new sciences an inner consistency or pattern which, when understood and made part of our intellectual systems, will enable us at least verbally to adjust ourselves to the new realities. But the most important level at which our new knowledge needs to be made part of us is at the level of day-to-day living and thinking and feeling—at the level of evaluations and orientations. For this task we need new images—as Gyorgy Kepes said, "images and symbols which can truly domesticate the newly revealed aspects of nature."

The task of creating these images and symbols, then, is the urgent task of the artist and designer today. The great difficulty of this task lies in the fact that symbols adapted from the visible world of hills and houses and trees and flowers and faces can rarely, if ever, serve as the iconography of our new scientific knowledge. Our basic knowings are no longer of things and their properties, but of structures—usually inferential structures. In other words, events at nuclear, atomic, and molecular levels, cosmic-ray phenomena, and events at the level of the extremely large, as in astrophysics, are not visual experiences, but logic and mathematical derivations from instrument readings and hypotheses. These inferred structures and events are never directly experienced;

THE UNACKNOWLEDGED LEGISLATORS

they can only be visualized (if at all) through the construction of models (such as molecular models) or through special kinds of photography (for example, stroboscopic analysis).

How can one symbolize with paint or plaster or stone such a grim reality as radioactive fall-out? Dr. Hans Thirring tells us that, "War fought with radio-isotopes would be noiseless and unbloody, yet disastrous for the peoples involved. A kind of light ash rain would cover densely populated areas with an almost invisible layer of dust, the presence of which could be detected only by Geiger counters and would not be noticeable to the normal human senses. It would neither smell nor sting, nor would it cause any immediate effects. . . . If not warned by radiation detectors, people in a contaminated area might pursue unsuspecting their everyday activities, yet be doomed to die painful deaths within a few weeks or months."

From the summer of 1962, I recall the newspaper story of the eighteenth of a series of nuclear-bomb tests that occurred in the Pacific Ocean. It was not a big bomb according to present standards. It was described as being in the "low-megaton range," which means nevertheless that it was many, many times the size of the bombs that destroyed Hiroshima and Nagasaki. But imaginatively, most of us have lost any sense of the force and the terror involved in the release of this kind of destructive energy. The story of this explosion occupied about two-and-a-half column inches on page six of the newspaper in which I saw it. We were horrified when more than one hundred citizens of Atlanta lost their lives in a jet-plane accident in Paris. But we accept as routine the explosion of bombs that not only can, but are intended to, kill populations of one hundred thousand at once. Such is the callousness of imagination which most of us have developed.

Though the great Spanish artist Pablo Picasso was awarded a ten-thousand-dollar peace prize by the Soviet government, this same government does not permit the Russian people to view Picasso's paintings, which, according to orthodox Soviet critical standards, are decadent and degenerate. Because Picasso is an avowed Communist, the Soviet government honors his political views. But it protects the Russian people from his influence as an artist.

In America, however, we honor Picasso the artist. Big-circulation magazines devote pages to reproductions of his paintings. American collectors and museums pay tens of thousands of dollars for his paintings and sculptures, and every introductory course in the appreciation of modern art lingers over the study of his work. Yet, if an American begins to echo Picasso's political thinking, he will soon find himself deprived of his security clearance and his job and being queried by the House Un-American Activities Committee. What the Russians admire about Picasso, we censor; what we admire about him, the Russians censor. Nobody wants the whole Picasso.

The fact that we largely forbid the circulation of Communist ideas in violation of our declared principles of freedom of speech, while regrettable, is understandable in view of the tensions of the cold war. Both the Soviet Union and the United States, although to different degrees, restrict the freedom of the circulation of ideas thought to be dangerous to their existing regimes.

But when the Soviet government forbids the exhibition of Picasso's pictures, it is going beyond thought control to what might be called imagination control, which is perhaps in the long run a much more serious matter. Poets and artists are the antennae of a nation, sensing more quickly than politicians or generals the deepest needs of the people. If art is placed, as it is in the Soviet Union, in the service of the state, the artist can only express what politicians and generals have already perceived and felt—which means that the artist can no longer serve his function as the antenna, the detector of new tendencies, the seer. And this is the reason that so much of Soviet art is so dull and conventional—their paintings are often illustrations, rather than art: "Comrade Ivanov receiving Lenin Prize for increasing production in tractor factory."

The artist in America, then, remains free to perform as artist, rather than to function as propagandist or apologist for any existing order. He is free, therefore, to create those new symbols, however disturbing or strange they may appear on first glance, that will help to bring us emotionally to terms with our own times. The creation of these new symbols will require knowledge—not only knowledge of and insight into the new worlds of science, but also knowledge of an expanding concept of humanity as a rapidly changing world brings new contacts and new nations into our awareness and our lives. But most of all, the creation of a new symbolism will require courage—the courage to confront squarely the deep anxiety, for ourselves and for the future of humanity, that is the great dark cloud under which we are all destined to live for as many years as we can see ahead.

XII

COMMUNICATION AND THE

HUMAN COMMUNITY

MAN is, as Korzybski said, the time-binder, whose specific means of survival is communication not only among the living members of the species, but also from the dead to the living, from the living to generations yet unborn. Biologists have in recent years begun to view man in much the same way. Different creatures have, in the course of evolution, specialized in the development of a variety of survival mechanisms: man may be viewed, says J. Z. Young, the English anatomist who represents this point of view, as the creature whose specific technique of survival has been the development of means of communication—which includes the brain capacity to create the complex abstractions and symbolizations that make communication of other than primitive kinds possible. Young's special contribution is the light he throws on human societies and institutions and the symbols that unite them by viewing them as mechanisms for the organization of communication. In the Fifth Lecture of his book *Doubt and Certainty in Science*, he tells how, when looking at the Cathedral of Notre-Dame in Paris, he found tears in his eyes. Somebody, he felt, was communicating something to him by means of that great and beautiful structure. As a biologist interested in communication among animals and among human beings, he reflected hard and long on the questions: What is the cathedral communicating? What biological purpose does that communication serve? In trying to answer such questions as these, he arrived at a number of conclusions about human co-operation and communication which I, in turn, have filtered through my own evaluative screen and have reorganized. I wish to present here some conclusions I have arrived at since reading Young's great book.

A very early method of ensuring communication among people and creating societies, Young asserts, was what I shall call here "the Stage of Social Organization around a Physical Symbol." At first, Young conjectures, the symbol of society must have been a meeting place:

"In no other animal is the habit of assembly quite so well developed as it is in man. The biological significance of the habit is that by it the brain associations necessary for communications are formed. Some of the earliest of these [human] assemblies occurred at prominent hills of suitable shape, on and around which large numbers of people came together. One of the clearest pieces of evidence that we have about early social man is that he soon began to build large *artificial* hills. Objects nearly as big as anything we build now were the product of some of the early agricultural communities, nearly 10,000 years ago. Such huge objects are found all over the world—an English example is Silbury Hill in Wiltshire.

"I suggest that the value of building these objects was that they and their names were the signs by which men were trained to react to each other in such a way as to make society possible. At first, this must have been learned by all coming together at one place. Ritual feasting . . . [and other ceremonies] are occasions of training of the brains of the members of the community, so that they shall continue to react correctly, and hence get a living by cooperation and communication. Mankind has gone on assembling and building assembly places ever since. It is assuredly one of the features that the biologist should notice about him.

"The hill is a very convenient symbol because it is easy to ensure that the association is quickly formed. Everyone can stand or sit on the symbol while the ceremonies are performed. . . . But there are obvious disadvantages about large symbols too. If they are to act as signs for the whole of a big population it soon becomes hardly possible to get everyone on or in. You can, however, have a lot of rather smaller objects or temples, in place of the original natural holy mountain. Their construction may be reckoned as the first act of making tools of communication, the direct ancestor of television engineering we might say. . . ."

The reader has no doubt been reminded by these lines, as I have, of other instances of social organization around physical symbols; the Indian burial mound; shrines, churches, and temples; the Ark of the Covenant of the Old Testament. It would be justifiable, too, I think, to classify the organization of societies around kingships—a living individual, or a dynasty of living individuals—as another form of the utilization of physical symbols for creating social cohesion.

Next in the history of human co-operation and communication came what I shall call "the Stage of Social Organization around Verbal Symbols." Let me quote again from Young: ". . . each temple has its own spirit. How then can all temples serve as a means of association for a large group? At some stage arose the habit of speaking of a single god, resident not in one but in many temples. This was a discovery of very great power. The peoples who first learned it produced one of the greatest of human advances."

Indeed, it was a great advance to go from the physical to the verbal symbol, for the separate temples at Miletus and Rome and Carthage and Athens could then be *defined* as the dwelling places of *one* God, *whose spirit is everywhere*. In short, progress from the physical to the verbal symbols enabled social organization among people who lived much too far apart ever to meet in one place for an annual ritual memorializing their solidarity. Everyone who acknowledged the *name* of the one God and the appropriate beliefs and dogmas that went with that acknowledgment could be recognized as belonging to the same community.

But it was not easy to transfer loyalties from tangible and visible, and usually geographically fixed, physical symbols to more abstract verbal symbols. Long-established semantic habits had to be uprooted, and there must have been many for whom the transition was too much. (When the Japanese Crown Prince, now Emperor Hirohito, paid an official visit to England in 1920 in the course of an unsuccessful attempt to renew the then expiring Anglo-Japanese treaty of alliance, he broke precedent by being the first member of the Imperial family to set foot outside of Japan. Several patriots committed suicide as a gesture of protest against this journey, apparently feeling that the Imperial family "belongs" on Japanese soil.) As Young says: ". . . [I]t seems at first quite illogical. The model stretches credulity so far that, like many new abstractions it seems on the face of it absurd. How could one person live in many places? An example of this was the dilemma of David when driven out of Israel to live among the Philistines. His god was associated with the particular soil from which he had been expelled, so he felt separated from his god and actu-ally—and this is the point—he felt unable to worship him.

Naaman overcame a similar difficulty by carrying two sacks of hallowed soil with him on a mule. But the real solution of the problem came by emphasis on the name of the god. . . . The worship of the name of one god, not associated with any particular place, was surely the symbol that provided the cement for the next stage of human evolution, in which we partly still are."

(Naaman's story is told in the Second Book of Kings. He was a Syrian who came to Elisha to be cured of leprosy. The cure being successful, he said, "Behold, now I know that there is no God in all the earth, but in Israel. . . . And Naaman said, Shall there not then, I pray thee, be given to thy servant two mules' burden of earth? for thy servant will henceforth offer neither burnt offering nor sacrifice unto other Gods, but unto the Lord." Elisha's feelings about holy soil apparently continue to exist in our times. The following is from a letter in Abigail Van Buren's column in the San Francisco *Chronicle* of April 6, 1956: "Dear Abby: I room with a guy from Fort Worth, Texas, and he is perfectly sane in most respects BUT he keeps a box of dirt in his closet. This is just plain, ordinary dirt, but it is soil from his 'beloved Texas,' and he treats it like it was 'holy land.' We are really worried about him. Is this behavior normal?—RON.")

Age-old sentiments of affection for a central meeting place exist to some degree in all of us to this day. Mohammedans turn to their central meeting place, Mecca, when they pray, and try to visit the city before they die. Roman Catholics, too, like to visit Rome. Christian Scientists have a special feeling for Boston, as Mormons do about Salt Lake City. In 1953, when my wife, eldest son (then seven), and I visited Japan, my father (who is no more Shintoist than I am) took us in the course of our sight-seeing to Isé, the location of the most sacred of Shinto shrines. There my father paid the customary fee and reported our names to the priest in charge. There followed a strange and beautiful ceremony of music, dance, and prayer, in the course of which "the Haya-kawa family of Chicago, U.S.A." was duly reported in to the gods. Although unbelievers, we found it difficult to remain un-moved.

But Christian missionaries, both Catholic and Protestant, taking full advantage of the abstractive capacity of the verbal symbol, have also long known how to consecrate a meeting place in the wilderness by connecting it, through prayer, with the rest of Christendom. Thus monotheism overcomes, through the process of abstraction, the geographical limitations usually imposed by specific places of assembly as symbols of social cohesion. Nevertheless, the feeling that God is somehow closely associated with our place of birth—which is also the place where we first experienced the sense of membership in a society—dies hard. It is revealed in the expression "this godforsaken place," which means any place where you feel homesick and unhappy, and also in the expression "God's country," which means home—especially after you have been away for a long time.

The high point in Western monotheistic culture, which I have called the Stage of Organization around Verbal Symbols, was, as Young says, the Middle Ages. Speaking still as a biologist studying the communication systems of the human species, he writes: "The rule by which brains had functioned in the Western world in the middle ages was to describe every-thing that was observed in terms of religious symbols. By this convention of speech and writing all human experience and action was [sic] unified. It was an efficient brain system, pro-ducing a well-organized society and reasonably stable conditions. . . ."

Young does not mention the Mohammedan world, but it, too, was organized largely around verbal Master Symbols, reaching a high point in the eighth century, when the Saracen

Empire reached from Spain to Mongolia, and still another high point in the Ottoman Empire in the sixteenth century. The T'ang Empire, stretching from the China coast to the Caspian Sea in the seventh century, and the Byzantine Empire, which reached its climax in about the tenth century, are further instances of great societies formed by a combination of these early principles of organization, which means by the creation of common semantic reactions among large and scattered populations to certain Master Symbols—these symbols being as a rule the person of an emperor or king or pope, who in turn symbolizes an abstract principle that explains to the people the basis of their unity. At this stage there is, of course, no separation between church and state. Why should there be, when the emperor is also the Son of Heaven? The ruler of England is still the titular head of the Church of England, however anachronistic the title has become.

Useful as this principle of social organization around Master Symbols has been for thousands of years, there were limits beyond which it could not be extended, as the decline of the great empires of the past amply attests. These limits were probably set by the technical limitations of communication. With messages carried by horseback, on foot, or by sailing vessel, it is remarkable that the empires of the past ever managed to become as large as they did. (In view of such studies of communication and social structure as Nicholas Rashevsky's *Mathematical Theory of Social Behavior* and Karl Deutsch's *Nationalism and Social Communication,* I look forward to better explanations of the decline of great empires than the commonplace explanations in terms of "degeneration" and "moral decay." When was the world *not* going to the dogs?) But there are other than physical limits to this principle of organization.

What the great religions and empires and religious empires have in common, as I have said, is that they organized communication and co-operation among large groups of people often far removed from each other by having them share common semantic reactions to extremely general Master Symbols. As in the earlier, tribal methods of social organization, however, they relied basically upon the creation of what sociologists call an in-group—which means that by the very act of so doing, an out-group is also defined. Just as you knew in a prehistoric culture that the man you met once a year at the Great Burial Mound was a fellow tribesman and therefore one with whom you could safely communicate, so you knew in the stage of the great empires that the man who paid his respects to the same Master Symbols that you respected was someone it was safe to talk to. We have all read those conversations in the *Arabian Nights* which begin, "Allah is great!" to which the other person replies, "Allah is indeed great!" After these preliminaries, communication begins. Suppose, however, the second person in response to the greeting "Allah is great!" replies, "Jesus is my Savior"?

In short, at the stage of social development represented by the great religions and empires (in Western civilization, the Middle Ages), the human race is inevitably divided into the in-group, the believers, and the out-group, the unbelievers, the infidels, the lesser breeds without the law—with whom communication is by definition impossible, or, at best, improbable.

Next, then, there is the latest stage in the development of human co-operation and communication, which I shall call "the Stage of Organization around Shared Perceptions." This is perhaps the greatest advance of all in the history of human communication. The basic idea of this new stage was clearly understood by many of the ancient Greeks.

Let me present a communication characteristic of the stage of shared perceptions, quoted from Strato, one of Aristotle's successors in the headship of the Lyceum at Athens, who occupied that position from 287 to 269 B.C.:

"We must first correct a popular illusion. It must be clearly grasped that vessels which are generally believed to be empty are not really empty but are full of air. Now air, in the opinion of the natural philosophers, consists of minute particles of matter for the most part invisible to us. . . . To prove this make the following experiment. Take a seemingly empty vessel. Turn it upside-down, taking care to keep it vertical, and plunge it into a dish of water. Even if you depress it until it is completely covered no water will enter. This proves that air is a material thing which prevents the water entering the vessel because it has previously occupied all the available space. . . . If . . . you lift the vessel vertically out of the water and turn it up and examine it you will see that the interior of the vessel has remained perfectly dry. This constitutes the demonstration that air is a bodily substance."

What is important to notice in Strato's method of communication is that, instead of saying, "Listen, friend, since I acknowledge the same god as you, you know that you can believe me when I say that air is a material substance," he says, "You don't have to take my word for it; you can see for yourself." As Benjamin Farrington says, in *Greek Science II*, in a scientific statement "a confirmatory action is demanded of the listener, a repetition of the experience." Such a statement is what we call in semantics "operational," in that it describes an operation the listener can perform to see for himself whether or not it is true. No doubt people had been making operational statements for thousands of years before Strato came along, but what is important in the Greek scientists, including Aristotle in those writings in which he writes as a scientist, is the fact that they tried *systematically* to make publicly confirmable, and only publicly confirmable, statements about selected areas of experience in order to organize knowledge and make it more readily communicable and usable. These systematic attempts on the part of the ancient Greeks are the foundations of Western science. Strato and Theophrastus and others like them were fifteen hundred years or more before their time, but without their contributions the scientists of the early Renaissance would have had even less intellectual capital with which to start.

The significant thing about Strato's way of communicating from our point of view is that it transcends local or regional loyalties and makes intercultural communication possible. In other words, what Strato says about air makes equal sense whether addressed to Greeks, Christians, Mohammedans, Hindus, or Australian aborigines. Anybody anywhere who has access to a jug and some water can see for himself whether or not Strato is right. And Strato's example of scientific communication is still, in principle, scientific communication today. The scientist today says, "If you will use the same language I use, perform the operations I have performed, and compute your results by the same mathematical system with which I compute, you will come to the same conclusions I came to. If you do not, let us compare what we did, step by step, and find out what misunderstanding of terms, what differences in the conditions of the experiment, what errors on your part or mine, caused the difference in the results. Then, when we have agreed on our conclusions, let us keep in communication with each other and proceed to other experiments. In this way you and I can help each other to know more and more about the world."

Now the great revolution implied in the transition from the Stage of the Master Symbol to the Stage of Shared Perceptions is that while in the former, agreements at high levels of abstraction (about God, about the Transmigration of Souls, about the Divine Right of Kings, and so on) were the basis of agreements at lower levels of abstraction, in the latter the reverse is the case. In order to share perceptions, we have to agree about obvious and even trivial things before agreeing about more general things. We have to collect verifiable observations about a variety of foods and diets and their effects on thousands of individuals before we can make a general statement about nutrition, and even then, we leave our general statement open to revision in the light of later observation. Systematic agreement about the properties of wood, water, metals, air, gases, has to be established before we can talk about matter in general. True enough, science sometimes makes a long extrapolation beyond the confirmable facts, as in the case of the theory of evolution, but that extrapolation is not accepted into the body of science until many more facts are adduced in its support. Science then, proceeds from agreements at lower levels of abstraction, step by step, to higher levels.

The caution and the so-called "objectivity" with which science proceeds, far from indicating the amorality of science, indicates its profound sense of social responsibility. The true scientist is so responsible to the rest of human society, including people of nationalities and religions different from his own, that he is unwilling to go beyond what *anybody* similarly trained in observation can confirm. If the scientist holds in check his preference for monogamy over polygamy, for private enterprise over collectivism, for his own national culture over other cultures, he does so not because he is indifferent to these issues, but because he feels that these are subjects about which publicly confirmable statements cannot *yet* be made, and because he wants above all, as a responsible communicator, to maintain the optimum conditions of communication with everybody, including those who may have different preferences as regards marriage customs, economic systems, or patriotic loyalties. He knows that to intrude the preferences of his own culture into his scientific discourse is to cut off his usefulness as a communicator to some segment of humanity. Does this mean that the scientist will forever refrain from making statements about disputed points of conduct or of social organization? Indeed it does not. It means merely that he is waiting until his statements about such matters can be put in confirmable form. Actually, scientists in the psychological and social sciences have already gone quite far in their attempts to throw light on problems of conduct and public affairs formerly settled by habit, intuition, or dogma; for example, in such areas as child care, psychology, psychiatry, criminology, and industrial management, the storehouse of confirmable and confirmed statements is steadily being added to.

The act of communication, says Anatol Rapoport in *Operational Philosophy,* is the basic moral act. The morality of the tribal stage insists that by regular participation in appropriate rituals at a common meeting place you maintain communication and co-operation with all the fellow members of your tribe. ("Go to church this Sunday!") The morality of the Stage of Master Symbols insists that, by the acknowledgment of more abstract symbols accepted in common by thousands or even millions who share those symbols with you, you maintain communication and co-operation with all your co-religionists. The morality of the Stage of Shared Perceptions insists that you try to maintain communication and co-operation with everybody, by basing your communications on the similarities in human nervous systems and the similarities of the experience of those nervous systems in their encounters with the observable world. One begins with the sharing of perceptions about commonplace or even obvious things, so that, with the establishment of myriads of little agreements, larger and larger agreements become possible.

Each of the three stages is moral, in that each is a method

of establishing and ensuring co-operation. Each requires the forgoing of egotistic drives in the interests of the larger group. For man is a social creature, which means that he is an incurably moral creature, finding his fulfillment only as he relates meaningfully and is in communication with a society.

Today we are largely in transition from concepts of morality inherited from the Stage of Master Symbols to newer concepts of morality and social responsibility implicit in the Stage of Shared Perceptions. This means, then, that the vast struggles going on in the world today are incorrectly thought of if they are described as the struggle of moral people (we) versus immoral people (they)—or, as the children phrase it from watching Westerns on television, the good guys versus the bad guys. What is struggling to emerge out of the great moralities of the Stage of Master Symbols, no longer adequate as principles of human organization in a world suddenly made tiny by technological advances in transportation and communication, is the even more general and all-embracing morality of the Stage of Shared Perceptions.

The emergence of this new morality is slow, because we are all struggling under the weight of sackloads of the holy soil of Israel, unable, like Naaman, to understand that it is possible to love and to pray without them.

XIII

THE GREAT BOOKS IDOLATRY

AND KINDRED DELUSIONS

THE crippling effect on the sackfuls of the earth of Israel which present-day Naamans insist on carrying around is apparent in a number of contemporary schools of thought which express, in one way or another, deep yearnings for the re-establishment of what they call a unitary society—a kind of society usually described with great eloquence as having order, homogeneity, and an agreed-upon set of values. These schools of thought differ among themselves in details, but there is sufficient similarity in their views so that we may, for the purposes of the present argument, lump them together under the general heading of the "New Conservatism." Not all of them go as far as T. S. Eliot, who, discussing the desirability of maintaining "tradition" and "orthodoxy," asserted in *After Strange Gods* that "What is . . . important is unity of religious background; and reasons of race and religion combine to make any large number of free-thinking Jews undesirable. . . . And a spirit of excessive tolerance is to be deprecated." But they are united in deploring the cultural pluralism and the heterogeneity of modern life, which they usually describe as "chaos and confusion." In deploring "chaos and confusion," they are not simply regretting the fact that most people and nations have not yet learned to settle their differences in an orderly way. They mean, rather, that the very fact that people are different in religion, politics, and value systems is to be deplored. The New Conservatives are all much alike, therefore, in their nostalgia for supposedly happier times in the past, when, because of geographical isolation and the difficulties of travel, there were few cultural or ideological differences to worry about.

Among the most influential and widely discussed philosophers and educators of this general persuasion in the past couple of decades have been what I like to call the "Neo-Neo-Scholastics," or the "Neo-Scholastics with neon lighting." The most dazzling of these sources of illumination have been, of course, Robert M. Hutchins and Mortimer J. Adler, the Divine Doctors of the Great Books Movement. It was (and presumably remains) their conviction, which they were able to persuade others to share through the expenditure of large amounts of foundation money, that the salvation of modern civilization lies in "restoring to their rightful place as the first principles of discourse and moral judgment the great and permanent values of Greek and Christian tradition." We shall recover those values, so we were told, by the conscientious study of the Great Books of the Western world.

In questioning this basic premise of the Great Books Movement, I am not, of course, arguing against the heritage of ancient Greece or of Christianity—which, I am sure, are at least as valuable as the heritage of ancient China or of Buddhism. What I am concerned with is the belief of Hutchins and Adler that agreements at the level of "first principles"—in other words, agreements at the highest possible levels of philosophical abstraction—are the *necessary condition* of intellectual, political, moral, and social order. As Hutchins wrote in *The Higher Learning in America,* "If we can revitalize metaphysics and restore it to its place in higher learning, we may yet be able to establish rational order in the modern world as well as in the universities." Get the metaphysics straight, so the argument goes, and everything else will turn out all right. Given such a premise, we are right back to that stage of social development which I have called the Stage of Organization around Master Symbols, in which, as in medieval Europe, metaphysical agreement was, at least officially, the foundation of all other agreements.

Another array of neon lights of Neo-Scholasticism is provided by *Time, Life,* and *Fortune,* which seem to have a central cadre of editorialists whose task it is to expound the metaphysics of the Luce empire. That metaphysics is sternly otherworldly; it asserts repeatedly that the basic questions confronting man are religious. It sternly opposes pragmatism, positivism, and excessive reliance upon science. In an Easter editorial in 1959, for example, *Life* excoriated "secularism," which "refuses on principle to ask questions which science cannot answer"; this nonreligious view, the editors asserted, is responsible for "the triviality and self-indulgence of American life."

[In view of how strongly the editors of *Life* feel about the triviality and self-indulgence of American life, one wonders how they could bring themselves to include in the same issue page after page of expensive and attractively laid-out advertising for Pontiac ("personal attention to quality is the secret of giving the customer a car he'll enjoy"); Soft-Weve ("the 2-ply tissue by Scott, the most noticed little luxury he'll enjoy"); and a spread of three full pages to say that Marlboros are obtainable either in soft pack or flip-top box. The reader is left quite at a loss as to what *Life* wants him to do: (1) to accept God and give up secularism and self-indulgence, or (2) to order a new Pontiac.]

Fortune, for all its glorification of mighty machines and huge business enterprises, also asserts a metaphysical position, namely, that the alternative to the moral confusion created by philosophically wrongheaded individuals such as Justice Oliver Wendell Holmes is "to spread across the American sky the news that the Law by which we seek to live, however imperfect a copy it may be, is nevertheless grounded in the Law of the Universe." If the legal profession, says Henry R. Luce, in *Fortune,* June, 1951, is properly to serve its function, it must declare "what is forever true"—and this must be done "before it is too late." Distress concerning the allegedly pernicious influence of Justice Holmes and a preoccupation with "Natural Law," usually so capitalized, are almost certain indices of the kind of Neo-Scholasticism I am attempting to describe. "Natural Law" (not to be confused with laws naturalistically derived) is a body of irrefutable moral principles laid down by God (according to the theistically inclined among the Neo-Scholastics) or discoverable in the laws of the universe or of human nature or of reason (according to nontheists). The duty of judges becomes, in a characteristic exposition of the theory by Walter Berns, in *Freedom, Virtue, and the First Amendment,* not simply the adjudication of cases brought before the courts, but the evaluation of laws—including the Constitution itself—in the light of "justice and virtue." As he writes, "The purpose of the Supreme Court cannot be described as making justice conform to the Constitution. It is rather to make the Constitution conform to justice."

Even more explicit in its metaphysics is *Time.* In its thirtieth anniversary issue (March 9, 1953), with a solemnity suitable to the occasion, *Time* dedicated itself sternly in a five-page editorial to the task of unconfusing the confusion of ideologies in the modern world by getting us all back to the "Great Truths of Western Civilization," which have been more and more neglected since the thirteenth century A.D.

The central problem of our age, said the editors of *Time*, is the crisis among intellectuals. Public opinion is able to arrive at right decisions only if there is "a certain agreement on moral standards, a framework of philosophy about man, the world, and the truth in which facts relevant to the news can be assembled, tests applied, and rational debate carried on." But as *Time* put the question, "In the U.S. today, is there enough unity about fundamentals to make for a sensible and fruitful debate on public policies? Are the limits of debate and the final standards of policy clearly and generally understood? To clarify such fundamentals is the duty of the intellectuals, especially the philosophers." But the philosophers are not, it appears, doing their job: "How true is the cliché that this is a time of 'growing intellectual confusion'? . . . like most clichés, it is all too true. . . . Today the idea of an objective, unchanging moral law is hotly denied by many social scientists, defended by other intellectuals and by a lot of nonintellectuals. . . . So intellectual confusion has been growing."

Once we are past these neon lights of Neo-Scholasticism, we are reminded of those night clubs in which the brilliance of the lights on the marquees outside is out of all proportion to the darkness within. As our eyes grow accustomed to the gloom, we discern an array of dim bulbs—such writers as:

Pitirim Sorokin, of Harvard, who believes that all people working on practical problems of society—politicians, social workers, welfare commissions, committees of international cooperation, et cetera—are wasting their time, since they haven't taken the trouble first to agree on the Eternal Values of the Kingdom of God.

Eliseo Vivas, philosopher at Northwestern University, who argues in a book called *The Moral Life and the Ethical Life* that the moral life must be informed by ethical insight, which rests upon acceptance of the fatherhood of God and the spiritual nature of man.

Sebastian de Grazia, author of *Errors of Psychotherapy,* who, although not a psychologist or psychiatrist—he is said to be a political scientist—says that psychotherapists of all kinds do not know what they are doing, and that the true treatment of emotional disorder is the reorganization of society ("The government within must be patterned after a government without"), which in turn depends on society's acceptance of a higher spiritual authority.

Allen Tate, poet, critic, and Catholic convert, who yearns for the good old days in the Old South, when gentlemen were gentlemen and the world was yet uncorrupted by science, modernism, liberalism, positivism, and carpetbaggers, and who, in the course of a controversy in 1949, added a new note to literary criticism in America by challenging his opponent to a duel.

Richard Weaver, of the University of Chicago, author of a book called *Ideas Have Consequences,* which bewails the "lack of responsibility" in the modern world and states that even fascism is preferable to liberal democracy, because, although fascism compels only a "harsh military responsibility," that is better than no responsibility at all.

Russell Kirk, contributor to *National Review,* editor of an ultraconservative quarterly called, for reasons not clear to me, *Modern Age,* and author of several books including a curious one called *Academic Freedom,* which argues that scholars in the Middle Ages enjoyed greater academic freedom than other scholars since that time, because they agreed on basic truths. How this kind of freedom differs from thought control is also not entirely clear to me.

Eric Voegelin, of Louisiana State University, upon whose book *The New Science of Politics* was based the solemn editorial in *Time* already referred to, who traces all modern disasters, including the Cromwellian revolution, political liberalism, welfare states, the rise of fascism, the menace of Russia, the triumph of Communism in China, and the rapid demobilization of American forces after World War II, to the baleful influence of a visionary twelfth-century monk called Joachim of Floris, who, we are asked to believe, handed down, to our vast misfortune, certain almost-forgotten pernicious teachings of the Gnostics of the second century, A.D.

(What the Gnostics taught that was so subversive and dangerous remains obscure to me in spite of the explanations of Voegelin, *Time,* and the 11th edition of the *Britannica.* Joachim of Floris, or Flora, c. 1145-1202, was a saintly monastic who prophesied that after the Age of the Father and the Age of the Son, there would be, starting in 1260 A.D., the Age of the Spirit, in which the whole world would be a vast monastery in which the ecclesiastical hierarchy, no longer necessary, would efface itself. Although his orthodoxy was affirmed by papal bull in 1220, certain Franciscan followers of Joachim used his ideas as a basis for an attack on the papacy, so that his writings later fell under condemnation. The connection between Joachim's ideas and the troubled modern world, as traced by Voegelin, to the awe and admiration of the editors of *Time,* can be followed if one is willing to be a victim of what psychiatrists call "clang associations." Joachim's vision of a purified world in his "Age of the Spirit" is, according to this view, the precursor of all attempts to establish the Kingdom of Heaven on earth—which is the arch-conservative's description of attempts, however modest, to improve man's condition of *this* world, rather than in the hereafter. Hence, Joachim is the spiritual father—hang on tight!—of such calamities as Calvinism, the French Revolution, the New Deal, and welfare states. Joachim's "third stage" of history, by this "reasoning," is the direct inspiration of Hitler's Third Reich, as well as of the Marxist idea of the three stages of social development from primitive communism to class-stratified societies to the classless society.

Since I, too, have divided human history into three stages for the purposes of argument, I am afraid I must be classed as a Joachimite. The reader, if he continues reading, does so at his own risk.)

What is it that these Neo-Scholastics are saying? In order to answer this question I should like to remind the reader of an incident in John Steinbeck's *The Grapes of Wrath*, in which a filling-station man continues to ask the same question over and over again after Casey has tried three times to answer it. Tom Joad, who has overheard the colloquy, finally loses patience: "Casey tries to tell ya an' you jest ast the same thing over. I seen fellas like you before. You ain't askin' nothin'; you're jus' singin' a kinda song. . . . Maybe you'll die pretty soon, but you won't know nuthin'. Just sing yourself to sleep with a song. . . ." In other words, Joad perceived that the man was simply making autistic noises and was therefore neither communicating nor inviting communication. The Neo-Scholastics of our time can be justly compared, I think, to the filling-station man. They are largely making autistic noises; they are neither communicating nor inviting communication. They're just singin' a kinda song, hence they won't know nuthin' and don't want to know nuthin'.

As my own contribution to knowledge, I should like to identify that song so that my readers will recognize it when they hear it again. I am tempted to call it the philosophers' version of Bessie Smith's "Empty Bed Blues." ("Woke up this mornin', when the chickens were crowin' for day./Look on the right side of my pillow, my man had gone away.") The following is a summary of the kind of blues the Neo-Scholastics sing:

Stanza I

The world is in chaos and confusion. It is in confusion because there is disagreement among intellectuals as to basic metaphysical principles; some don't even have principles. Intellectual confusion leads to confusion in political and moral leadership, which leads to confusion in the community and in family life. Alas.

Stanza II

Things were different in the thirteenth century. Philosophy was then recognized for what it is, the Queen of the Sciences. Plato and Aristotle were held in unquestioned reverence. Universal agreement on first principles resulted in a responsible aristocracy, a noble military, a contented peasantry, and tradesmen knew their places.

Stanza III

But today philosophical authority is no longer recognized. Most people have succumbed to the pernicious belief that any man's opinion is as good as anyone else's. This condition of intellectual anarchy is aided and abetted by scientists, pragmatists, positivists, relativists, and teachers colleges. Our schools teach everything from social dancing to safety education, but fail to meet the greatest responsibility of education, which is to teach first principles. Students are permitted to choose their courses instead of being required to study what is good for them. Hence there is no real education any more. Intellectual relativism leads to moral relativism, so that there aren't any morals any more either.

Stanza IV

Western civilization is rushing headlong toward barbarism. If intellectual leaders do not get back to the Eternal Truths of Greek and Christian tradition such as were the basis of medieval unity, our culture is doomed. Maybe it is doomed already, but don't say we didn't warn you.

I hope it is clear why I say that the Neo-Scholastics are merely singin' a song and neither communicating nor inviting communication. I am here not concerned with disputing their religious convictions, nor do I question their right to entertain as "first principles" whatever principles they wish to hold. What I do dispute is their basic contention that communication is impossible unless we *first* agree to accept *their* religious and metaphysical principles as the basis of discourse. They are saying in effect, "How can we communicate at all—how can we even agree as to what we are disagreeing about—unless we have a prior agreement and understanding about first principles?"

Believing, then, that communication in the modern world is impossible, the Neo-Scholastics yearn for the restoration of that stage of social organization which I have called the Stage of the Master Symbols. They realize, of course, that this method of organization has been in decline for a long time—since the thirteenth century so far as the Western World is concerned. Hence they are not at all sanguine about the realization of their hopes—which is reason enough to sing the blues. But what they do not realize is that ever since the invention of printing, the organization of society by the creation of common semantic reactions to Master Symbols has ceased to be the chief or even the most efficient method of organizing large societies.

Printing, more than any other single technological advance, liberated man from the stage of culture best illustrated in Western history by the Middle Ages. With the increased availability of books, people began to study the Scriptures for themselves and to interpret for themselves what they had previously relied upon a priestly elite to interpret for them.

This proliferation of private interpretations of the Scriptures meant, of course, the emergence of one Protestant sect after another—a process of division which continues in Protestantism to this day. The authority of Rome over the whole of Western civilization was ended.

Furthermore, because of the rapid spread of literature made possible by printing, people not only had the opportunity to exchange information and compare notes; they also had to develop the skills necessary to weigh the comparative merit of conflicting opinions and reports. Thus was developed the habit of critical reading—the habit of putting one's trust not so much in the writer who exhibited the most impressive array of authority symbols as in the writer whose statements were most thoroughly confirmed by one's own experience and observation. Strato's way of communicating began to come into its own.

Printing, which was the greatest advance in the arts of communication since the invention of writing and until the advent of electronics, slowly but radically changed people's attitudes and patterns of evaluation. It democratized knowledge, hence rendered unnecessary those attitudes of reverence for one's betters and sensitivity to social status that, in an earlier stage of human culture, were the cement of social cohesion. The Neo-Scholastics constantly bewail the absence of hierarchy and authority in the world today. If books could be made as scarce as Rolls-Royces, as they were in the Middle Ages, and if the literacy rate could be reduced again to something like one or two per cent, the Neo-Scholastics would be entitled to have their wish for the restoration of a hierarchical society, since it would make sense.

Can the Stage of Social Organization around Master Symbols ever be restored? None but the Neo-Scholastics believe so, and, as I have indicated, even they don't believe it very strongly, or else they wouldn't sound so unhappy most of the time. However, by a sufficiently unscrupulous use of force and fraud and rigid censorship, Nazi Germany and Communist Russia did succeed in establishing societies organized around Master Symbols in modern times. The "Heil Hitler" salute and the ideological commitments symbolized by that gesture were, in Nazi Germany, the necessary preconditions of communication. Those who did not acknowledge fealty to these Master Symbols were beaten, jailed, exiled, or killed.

The reader will recall, too, what happened to the science of genetics in the Stalinist era in Russia with the ascendance of T. D. Lysenko. Lysenko replaced the type of statement that says, "My genetic theory is true: you can confirm it for yourself by experiment," with an altogether different kind of statement, "My genetic theory is true because it has the Good Housekeeping Seal of Approval of the Central Committee of the Communist Party." However, by so doing, Lysenko closed down the Iron Curtain over the science of genetics.

The foregoing are my reasons for asserting that the Neo-Scholastics are not seriously interested in communicating. Trying to restore the Master Symbol stage of human organization in the twentieth century is the negation of communication.

Even more seriously, the Neo-Scholastics are not inviting communication either. I should like to take up this charge in some detail, since in doing so I hope to be able to make clear the changes in evaluative habits brought about by profound changes in the conditions of communication.

A fundamental prejudice to be found in the entire Neo-Scholastic school of thought is the belief that sense perceptions and experience are irrelevant and immaterial to the pursuit of "true knowledge." "True knowledge," according to the point of view immortalized by Plato, is knowledge of "essences." "Essences" are not to be perceived by the physical eye; they are apprehended by an act of "pure intellectual intuition," *totally* independent of the senses. Every essence has a name; the description of the essence of a thing is called its "definition." Knowledge of definitions is therefore knowledge of essences, which is therefore knowledge of all you will ever need to know. Aristotle's view was somewhat less radical in that he seemed to believe that experience of physical things at least had the function of training the mind for the perception of essences. But ultimately the two were alike in holding that knowledge of definitions is knowledge. "Actual knowledge," as Aristotle put it, "is identical with its object." Hence, at the heart of medieval Scholasticism as of Neo-Scholasticism is a fantastic reverence for definition and a contempt for observation and extensional methods.

I should like to show that there is a way in which the reverence for definition and the contempt for physical experience make a weird kind of sense, given the conditions of a society governed by Master Symbols. Since communication requires a certain amount of agreement on vocabulary, the establishing of definitions as rules of language is an act of creating order out of linguistic chaos. Hence if you are trying to organize such a society, one of your first needs will be a group of scholars whose task it will be to tell people what names to use in referring to what objects and situations, so that communication will become possible.

In almost every society of the Master Symbol stage, therefore, in both the Western world and the Far East, there has been a priestly caste engaged in what might be called "dogmatic lexicography." Dogmatic lexicography does not, like modern scientific lexicography, *describe* the languages and dialects that people use; instead it *prescribes* a language for everybody to use. In Confucianism, for example, there is the Doctrine of the Rectification of Names, which means that if everybody understands what is meant by "king," "father," "servant," "soldier," "justice," "property," "theft," and so on, society itself will be well ordered.

The establishment of definitions is therefore not what Plato imagined it to be, an insight into Eternal and Transcendental Verities and the basis of all knowledge; it is, as the Confucians realized, a principle of social control. By elevating definitions, which are simply rules of language, to the status of a Doctrine of Essences, Plato hit upon a formula that in application would have made social control absolute and airtight. If the pronouncements of dogmatic lexicography are understood merely as rules of language, the rules might conceivably be changed with changing times. But, as is well known, Plato was against all change. Hence he regarded his definitions as final, changeable only by an act of sacrilege against the Divine Order.

Nevertheless, the danger remained that *observant* men might want to change the rules anyway. The world of nonverbal, physical reality is untidy and unpredictable; new facts are always turning up that do not fit snugly into preestablished categories; inconsistencies between official definitions and the actualities of events are always emerging. These observed discrepancies between definition and fact constantly threaten the permanence of definitions and therefore, it was thought, threaten the social order. Plato's formula was perfectly calculated to freeze a society forever: the masses would never question their high priests, and the high priests would never doubt the validity of their own definitions, if they both followed his demand that they disregard the evidence of their senses. In what David Riesman calls the tradition-directed society, in which change is slow and in which there are none but customary problems to be solved in ways long sanctioned by custom, Plato's formula was not necessarily suicidal. It was a formula for the complete arrest of human curiosity and intelligence, but curiosity and intelligence only get a man in trouble in Master Symbol societies, as Galileo was only one of many to discover.

Little wonder, then, that Plato's formula has been held in reverence ever since by high priests, would-be high priests, and by all, including the editors of *Time*, who dislike adjusting to change. Too much detailed practical information, so the formula goes, besides having the ignoble connotation that you might be an artisan, has the additional disadvantage of blurring one's insight into essences. Information is therefore to be avoided where possible and accepted only in small amounts when it can't be avoided. As Richard Weaver puts it in *Ideas Have Consequences*: "I shall adhere to the classic proposition that there is no knowledge at the level of sensation, and that therefore knowledge is of universals. . . . The fewer particulars we require in order to arrive at our generalization, the more apt pupils we are in the school of wisdom."

The contempt for observation and practical knowledge of all kinds arises too, of course, from a prejudice common to all societies in which there is a strongly entrenched mandarinate. The most cherished caste mark of intellectuals, priests, and the aristocracy is their exemption from labor. Aristotle definitely regarded working people as not human: "We think the manual workers are like certain lifeless things which act indeed, but act without knowing what they do, as fire burns." Even today, in some writings on "the education of free men," "free" means free of the necessity of working for a living. (Here again Richard Weaver's book can serve as an example, especially his furious attacks on "vocationalism" and "professionalism" in education, Ch. III.) In such contexts, the opposite of "free" is "servile," which is applied to those who work for a living—perhaps the most shameful thing a man can be forced to do in traditional hierarchical societies.

I should add here in fairness that Hutchins and Adler, along with *Time, Life,* and *Fortune,* while sharing the metaphysics of the Neo-Scholastics, do *not* share the antidemocratic views of the more rabid types among them. The every-man-a-philosopher program of the Great Books Movement is profoundly democratic in spirit, however mistaken in educational philosophy. The Luce magazines, too, believe in democracy and an enlightened public opinion; *Life*'s many series of excellent articles on nature, history, religion, and art can only be motivated by a genuine respect for the common man.

"I shall adhere to the classic proposition that there is no knowledge at the level of sensation. . . . The fewer particulars we require in order to arrive at our generalizations, the more apt pupils we are in the school of wisdom." This passage from Weaver sums up what I mean when I say that the Neo-Scholastics—the more moderate among them in theory, and the extremists among them in fact—do not even invite communication. They don't want to hear any facts; it's against their principles. They don't want to hear any first principles either, because they believe they already know all the first principles worth knowing. Hence, as I have said, they have a point of view that is resolutely and hopelessly anti-intellectual.

Norbert Wiener says in *Cybernetics: The Human Use of Human Beings* that, "Information is thus the name for the content of what is exchanged with the outer world as we adjust to it, and make our adjustments felt upon it. The process of receiving and of using information is the process of our adjusting to the outer environment, and of living effectively under that environment. . . . To live effectively is to live with adequate information." Instead of following Wiener's principles, the Neo-Scholastics would have us shut out information and employ as our basic means of problem-solving and survival only that fractional portion of our nervous system that is concerned with the mechanisms of verbalization. And since "there is no knowledge at the level of sensation," the operation of even that fractional portion must be completely unrelated to the rest of our nervous system: our wonderful senses of touch and sight and smell and proprioception.

In sum, these lost children of Naaman assert that verbalism unchecked by experience or observation is the basic principle of wisdom. They appear not to know that it is the basic principle of schizophrenia.

XIV

THE AIMS AND TASKS OF

GENERAL SEMANTICS

THE aims and tasks of general semantics, however numerous they may seem to be to the many students of the subject who are busy applying its formulations to the sciences, to humanistic studies, and to practical affairs in business or education, may all be regarded as parts of one large, all-embracing task, namely, that of advancing human time-binding. It is the task of students of general semantics first to bring to wider scientific and public awareness the fact of time-binding as the central mechanism of human survival. Secondly, it is their task as citizens to encourage and strengthen those cultural institutions—economic, political, or social—under which time-binding best flourishes, and to oppose those conditions which would discourage or limit time-binding. It is also their task to nurture through education or therapy or social engineering, those conditions of emotional maturity such as will ensure the fullest realization of the time-binding potential that resides in every human being.

Fitness to survive, for human beings, does not mean aggressiveness and ferocity, as it does for beasts of prey; nor does it mean the ability to outrun enemies, like the antelope or deer; nor building protective shells around oneself, like the oyster and the tortoise. Human fitness to survive means the time-binding capacity, that is, the ability to organize communication and co-operation. It means the ability to create language; it means the ability to systematize information so that it can be remembered and recorded and passed on to others; it means the ability to create societies, which are essentially complex networks of communication. Human beings are not limited to forming face-to-face groups, as are the gibbon and the chimpanzee; they possess the immeasurably more significant ability to organize social organization *at a distance* and *over generations of time.*

When human beings communicate with each other with jungle drums or with electromagnetic waves, they are behaving in ways specific to their species. When human beings make use of science, technologies, ethical systems, or literature, they are using the accumulated insights, intuitions, and observations of thousands of fellow-members of their species, most of them long since dead. Human beings also add to their knowledge and techniques from generation to generation, so that each generation can start where the last left off. The time-binding capacity is but another name for the ability to create civilizations.

All human cultures are the product of time-binding—of communication from the past to the present. Even the most primitive of living human beings speak languages with incredibly rich vocabularies and complex grammatical structures —languages inherited from earlier generations. Also inherited are almost all of their beliefs, myths, rituals, tools, skills, and patterns of social organization. Ancestor worship, which is to be found in the early stages of almost all known cultures, is primitive man's way of assuring that communications from tribal forebears shall be respectfully heeded, religiously memorized, and reverently passed on. Before the invention of writing, it was probably the best conceivable way of assuring the preservation and accurate transmission of accumulated knowledge.

The definition of man as time-binder is similar to the anthropologist's definition of man as culture-bearer in that both definitions place emphasis on the fact that men are social products, each human individual being a member of a society which includes not only his living contemporaries but the dead—the long line of his cultural ancestors. The two definitions differ, however, in that the former accepts *progress* as a measure of successful time-binding. Time-binding implies that when a culture is functioning well its resources become richer as time goes on: knowledge increases, technology improves, literary and artistic resources become more abundant. Time, says Korzybski, is the human dimension. Static cultures, in which generations may pass without change, are doomed cultures.

Nevertheless, all cultures throughout known history have placed limits on time-binding. First of all there is the ancient prejudice against communicating with or heeding communications from anyone other than one's own tribal group. By this orientation, if you are an Uzbek, you must not listen to un-Uzbekian ideas; if you are an American, you must not listen to un-American ideas. This prejudice we inherit from that stage of culture in which time-binding was largely within the tribal group, and in which the outsider, the worshiper of strange gods, was an object of fear.

Time-binding is also limited by the practice of most cultures of making tabu the investigation and discussion of certain topics. In some cultures, communication between classes and castes is severely restricted. Most cultures believe that on certain topics all that can be known or is necessary to know has already been accumulated; consequently those who might wish to question or add to that knowledge are persecuted. For example, in the Soviet Union, those who wish to question or correct the doctrines of Marx and Lenin are denounced as "revisionists." The fact that "revisionist" is a term of condemnation is itself a revelation of an anti-time-binding attitude. If no "revision" is permitted, no advance is possible either. To be sure, limitations of the time-binding process are themselves products of culture. But they run directly counter to the process by which culture is created.

The general semanticist, therefore, cannot go all the way with those cultural anthropologists who refuse to evaluate the relative merit of cultures. He is logically compelled to prefer those cultures which place few limitations on time-binding over those which place many. He is compelled to prefer those actions and measures which increase the total amount of time-binding over those which may decrease or arrest time-binding. For the definition of man as time-binder is a definition of man as a co-operative class of life; the more men co-operate, the more do they manifest their humanness.

Consequently, the student of general semantics, as a citizen, will tend to support ideals of international and cultural co-operation such as are held by people of good will, of many different faiths and nationalities, all over the world. He will tend to support the United Nations, which hopes to transcend the limited time-binding of separate and soverign nations with fuller time-binding on an international scale: the pooling of the material, technical, and intellectual resources of all the nations of the world for the purpose of solving problems wherever they may arise. He will tend to oppose political thought-control wherever it may arise, for thought-control is the antithesis of time-binding. He will oppose racial and religious discrimination, not solely out of democratic sentiment, but also out of a conviction that fullest time-binding necessitates the freest cultural interchange between all races and creeds and classes. He will support freedom of speech, press, and assembly not solely because he is culturally conditioned to value these freedoms (although this no doubt will be a large part of his reason), but also because he holds that restrictions of these freedoms are denials of the cultural process. The definition of man as a time-binder gives the general semanticist a theoretical basis upon which all cultures, including his own, may be criticized and evaluated.

Another way of looking at general semantics is to say that it is an intellectual method to enable us to apply scientific ways of thinking to everyday life, to problems of social interaction, to problems of decision in practical affairs, as well as to the critical analysis of problems in science or scholarship.

Science, in the view of students of general semantics, is the outstanding example of time-binding behavior. All problem-solving requires making some kind of more or less accurate "maps" of the "territories" we are dealing with. If we wish to build a bridge, we must know something about the properties of the materials used, the characteristics of the river to be bridged; if we wish to rule a nation, we have to know something about the people in it, their habits and desires, the resources available to meet their needs, and so on. Whether we successfully build the bridge or govern the nation depends on the adequacy of our map-making.

There are two facets to science: first, it is the systematization of certain habits common to at least a part of the problem-solving behavior of all people in all cultures, namely, observing, checking, making hypotheses, and testing them. Second, it is the systematization of methods whereby such perceptions may be shared. In order that any number of observers may communicate with each other and exchange reports, linguistic conventions, such as systems of scientific nomenclature and systems of weights and measures, are established. Thus, observations are compared, experiments are repeated, errors are corrected, and information is accumulated. Science is a huge co-operative enterprise of human beings jointly trying to make better and better maps of reality.

Extrascientific motives, such as commercial or military rivalry, often interfere with the free exchange of ideas and information so that in many areas scientists are not permitted to be as fully co-operative as they would like to be. Nevertheless, science offers the outstanding example in world history of international intellectual co-operation. The scientific world has institutionalized time-binding habits. It has also institutionalized the avoidance of those cultural or private habits of evaluation that hinder or limit time-binding. The culture pattern of the scientific world is therefore not just another culture pattern to be evaluated as no better and no worse than the kinship system of the Australian aborigines or the potlatch of the Kwakiutl. The culture pattern of the scientific world is, rather, the systematic selection from prevailing culture patterns of those specific ways of abstracting and those specific forms of linguistic behavior that ensure the maximum exchange of knowledge and the maximum of human agreement.

Science, then, is a technique of agreement, perhaps the greatest we have, and certainly the only one which has been strongly enough institutionalized among enough people in enough places and to have produced enough results to have acquired an almost universal prestige. Sometimes it is said that "science isn't everything," that "science is arrogant," that "science has become a sacred cow." Such comments appear to me to show an almost sinful blindness to what is central to science, which is, above all things, a technique of agreement that systematically seeks to reach across cultural divisions of race, language, religion, and social status, in order to extend the possibilities of human co-operation.

It is the position of general semanticists that the orientation of science, central to which is the determination to find grounds for agreement so that investigators may go on *together* from there, need not, indeed, cannot, be confined to scientists. Scientists themselves, to be sure, often fail to exhibit such an orientation outside the laboratory, nor are they uniformly successful in exhibiting it within. Nevertheless, the main features of this orientation are easily described. In addition to the desire for agreement, another feature of the scientific orientation is its essential democracy, which resides in the fact that all may contribute to science what they can and take from it what they need. A related feature of science is the fact that all scientific statements are always open to challenge.

In science, Wendell Johnson once said, there is never the last word, but the latest. Time-binding is a process without end. Conditions change, the earth changes, human needs change, the boundaries of knowledge change, so that even the most established of scientific truths inevitably need, sooner or later, modification or revision. A scientist must always retain his ability to listen, his ability to take in new information, or he ceases to be a scientist.

In advocating the *orientation* of science, then, the general semanticist is by no means saying that everyone should study physics, chemistry, or mathematics. It is possible for some people to spend a lifetime in the physical sciences without ever acquiring a scientific orientation about the generality of non-technical problems. The scientific orientation may be acquired with or without training in the sciences—indeed, people may acquire it without formal schooling at all. This orientation might have been called the "political orientation" or the "philosophical orientation" if it had been first institutionalized in politics or philosophy. Calling it the scientific orientation is simply recognition of the fact that science is so far the only human activity in which this orientation has been institutionalized.

In order to make clear what I mean by the scientific orientation, let me contrast it with some prescientific and antiscientific orientations. If people do not have the attitudes of an earnest desire for agreement, if they are not content with small agreements as a basis for building larger agreements later, if they are not willing to listen, if they do not have a respect for facts arrived at by any number of independent observers and the ability to modify or correct generalizations in the light of new information, what alternative attitudes are they likely to have?

First, there is the orientation of dependency, in which statements are accepted not because they are verifiable, not even because they are logically consistent, but because they originate from a parent or parent-surrogate, which may take the form of a person, a professor, an employer, a political leader, or, at a more abstract level, a philosophical system, a sacred book, or even a hundred sacred books. The general motto of this orientation may be stated as "Daddy says so." With this orientation, widespread human agreement would be possible if, and only if, everybody in the world accepted the same parent-figure as authority.

Throughout recorded history, people have realized that universal human agreement would be desirable; they have therefore tried to achieve it by trying to get people to agree on a common parent-figure. They have sought to conquer the world for Alexander, Ghengis Khan, Napoleon, and Hitler, in order that, when the conquest was over, universal peace would descend on the earth. People imbued with missionary spirit have operated on the same assumptions. Obviously if we all accepted Jesus, Buddha, Mahomet, or Father Divine, we would have a basis for universal agreement. However, people throughout history have never been able to agree on the acceptance of a common father-figure.

Another prescientific or antiscientific orientation is word mindedness—the tendency to verbomania—as distinguished from fact-mindedness. Among the unstated assumptions of this orientation are the following: "If a statement sounds true, it must be true"; "If it is eloquently stated, it must be true"; "If the speaker has a beautiful voice, it must be true"; also, "If a statement logically follows from self-evident truths, it must be true." Words are remarkably intoxicating. A flood of oratory is capable of producing a mild jag in most people; some orators, such as Adolf Hitler, have been able to produce much more than a mild jag.

In addition to the mass hysteria produced by demagogues, there is the more dignified kind of spellbinding among intellectuals produced by what may be called the scholastic tradition. The Greeks, an inexhaustibly loquacious people, seem to have started it. It was their assumption that if people argued and talked long enough about something, the truth would emerge. Putting statements to operational tests was something that rarely occurred to them, perhaps because they were not accustomed to using their hands, since they had slaves to do their work for them. The inheritors of this garrulous tradition do not, to this day, put propositions to operational tests—and we are all, in Western civilization, inheritors of this tradition. Therefore we all have within us, on some subjects, an excessive susceptibility to resounding and erudite phrases whose meaninglessness is obscured by their respectability in learned discourse.

Still another orientation is that of mysticism, which is usually an extreme form of verbomania. The mystic is one who talks to himself and others of a like mind in a language comprehensible only to himself, but which seems to give him great inward satisfaction. This language is usually extremely high-falutin', and often meaningless—in which case it is simply a symptom of verbomania. Sometimes, however, the language of the mystic appears to stand for something quite real in his experience, some kind of events or perceptions for which common language has no name, no vocabulary. In such a case, the mystic seems to be spraying a large number of words around at random in the hope that some of them will hit the target. And the hearer is always left with the question: Is there a target at all? If there is a target, what the mystic says today may be the subject of a science tomorrow. But the trouble with mystical language, whether or not it stands for something, is that it is incapable of producing human agreement. And the criticism to be made of most mystics is that they usually show little disposition toward revising their language in ways that might enhance the possibility of sharing their perceptions with others.

Another orientation alternative to the scientific is that of wishful thinking. According to this point of view, whatever we want passionately enough to be so is so. This orientation is one greatly encouraged by most of the major forces of public opinion—including especially the dream-factories of advertising and the movies. James Thurber's famous short story "The Secret Life of Walter Mitty" describes the absurd and unrealistic daydreaming of an ineffectual man. In the movie version of the story, the dreams are made to come true! (Mr. Thurber protested in vain the distortion of the meaning of his story.) The moral of the movie seems to be that we should all believe what we want to believe, no matter how improbable—and our faith will be rewarded. Many criticisms, political, economic, and psychiatric, can be made of this orientation, but for our present purposes it is sufficient to point out that it does not help the cause of widespread human agreement.

The last orientation alternative to the scientific that I wish to discuss is the "yes-but" orientation. This is the orientation of people who are willing to make verifiable statements, to seek languages in which agreement is possible, and in every way to behave like earnest time-binders *except* when they arrive at subjects involving their special moral, philosophical, cultural, or class prejudices, at which point they dig their heels into the ground and cry, "Yes, but . . ." This orientation is extremely common—I suspect we all have it to some degree—and no doubt it has been encouraged by the many crude misapplications of what looks like scientific method to areas where those particular scientific methods are not appropriate. The most dignified manifestation of this orientation is to be found in that philosophical position known as dualism, of which the classic motto is Ralph Waldo Emerson's, "There are two laws discrete . . . Law for man, and law for thing." Everything in the universe, except man, is discussable, according to this view, by science, which is the "law for thing." The "law for man," however, is something else, to be discussed by other methods. Now, this may well be true; there are indeed shortcomings to the so-called "objective" scientific method when we discuss human problems, especially our own. I shall not presume to say what Emerson meant by his statement, but those who make a motto of it use it to justify throwing out the scientific *orientation* as well as the method in discussions of human problems. Unfortunately, the other kinds of orientation—the Daddy-says-so orientation, the intensional orientation or orientation toward verbal autointoxication, the mystical orientation, and the orientation of wishful thinking—seem to be about the only existing alternatives. Hence philosophical dualists and other yes-butters are destined, at whatever point they say yes but, to have some area in their thinking in which their orientations preclude the possibility of widespread agreement.

What we call in general semantics a scientific orientation is not, therefore, test tubes, or logarithmic tables, or betatrons, or other paraphernalia of science; it is not even an attitude of cold, calculating detachment, as is popularly believed. (The notion that science and reason are of necessity "cold" is a superstition engendered by the fact that, since the more spectacular forms of unscientific behavior are obviously hot and impetuous, it is assumed that their opposite must be cold and detached. But extremely unscientific behavior can also be cold and detached—indeed, it can become routine—as anyone can testify who has seen at work the slow bureaucracy of railroad ticket offices.) The essentials of scientific orientation are simply (1) the determination to find bases of agreement and the concomitant degree of intellectual and emotional flexibility, (2) the willingness to put statements to operational test, and (3) the internalization of the knowledge that there is always something more to be learned about everything, so that one always remains capable of listening. In short, the orientations of science are simply the orientations of sanity; this is the meaning of the title of Korzybski's book *Science and Sanity*. Sanity, so defined, is necessary to every field of human activity.

The district in Chicago surrounding the University of Chicago is known as Hyde Park. Immediately to the north is the Kenwood neighborhood. The Hyde Park–Kenwood area was known in the late 1940's as a transitional area—which is a polite way of saying that it was on the road to becoming a slum. Faced with this fact, a number of concerned people, including Professor Herbert A. Thelen of the University's Department of Education, the Social Order Committee of the 57th Street Meeting of Friends, Rev. Leslie Pennington of the First Unitarian Church, Thomas Wright of the Mayor's Commission on Human Relations, Earl B. Dickerson of the Chicago Urban League, and Rabbi and Mrs. Jacob Weinstein and members of their congregation, started in 1949 an organization called the Hyde Park–Kenwood Community Conference. The purpose of the Conference was to stop neighborhood deterioration and the flight to the suburbs and to create, if possible, an interracial community that all its residents could continue to be proud of.

People living in a single block were the basic units in which the Conference was organized. The work began with block meetings—meetings of people who were mostly strangers to each other, as they are in large cities, but who were united by some common problem. In one block people were concerned about the many purse-snatchings that took place on their inadequately lighted street; in another block people were upset because Negroes had moved into one of the houses; in other blocks there were problems of unsatisfactory garbage removal, inadequate play space for small children, unsightly old cars abandoned on the streets, and illegal conversions of one-family residences into kitchenette apartments.

Certain well-tested rules were formulated by Professor Thelen for the conduct of discussion at these block and neighborhood meetings. Ideological discussions were strictly avoided; for example, whether in a democracy one should or should not segregate Negroes and whites. No attempt was made to change prejudices or to question basic attitudes. Meetings were devoted first of all to getting an accurate account of the conditions that people were concerned about. Investigating committees were appointed and sent out for more facts when information was lacking. Rumors were evaluated as rumors and not acted upon until verified. Since most rumors proved to be unfounded, the mere act of establishing the facts dispelled some of the anxieties that made the meetings necessary. Sometimes the allaying of false rumors had the effect of changing the minds of people who had impulsively decided to sell their property and move to the suburbs.

As a result of the activities of the Conference, interesting things began to happen in Hyde Park and Kenwood. Illegal conversions were slowed down and the city's building inspectors were put on notice that in Hyde Park and Kenwood at least they were expected to do their job of upholding standards. Many blocks set up neighborhood programs for the solution of parking problems, for street maintenance, and for recreation. In some blocks where city garbage collection had become lax and perfunctory since Negroes had moved in (such was the practice of the city's sanitation department), residents combined to demand the full restoration of services—and got it. Co-operative work sessions were organized to clean up vacant lots and make them into play areas for small children ("tot lots"). Together, the block organizations learned how to exert collective pressure on City Hall for better policing, better enforcement of zoning laws, and the general improvement of the community. The story of how the Conference operated is told in two fascinating books, *The Dynamics of Groups at Work* (1954), by Herbert A. Thelen, and *A Neighborhood Finds Itself* (1959), by Julia Abrahamson, who was executive director of the Conference during the first six years of its existence.

Professor Thelen gave a lecture in Chicago in 1954 in which he described the work of the Conference. A friend of mine remarked as he left the lecture hall, "By gosh, *that* is semantics in action!" Whether or not it is semantics in action (and I believe it is), the block meetings of the Hyde Park–Kenwood Conference were an impressive demonstration in action of the principles of communication of what I have called in an earlier chapter the Stage of Social Organization around Shared Perceptions. The whole secret of the Conference lay in starting discussion at the lowest levels of abstraction—at the level of concrete facts about street lighting, automobile traffic, play space, crowded living quarters—and going on to more general topics having to do with city ordinances, zoning laws, taxation, and the like.

(In contrast to the foregoing, there is the position of Richard Weaver, the Neo-scholastic philosopher of the University of Chicago whom I have already quoted in another connection. Asserting the necessity for metaphysical agreement before any other communication can be established, he says, "How can men who disagree about what the world is for agree about any of the minutiae of daily conduct?" His prescription apparently is to concentrate on the attainment of metaphysical agreement while letting the garbage accumulate—and when the accumulation becomes intolerable, to move to the suburbs, so that the suburbs become intolerable too.

The Conference got no help either from another of the neoscholastics of the University of Chicago. Julia Abrahamson writes:

"On March 17, 1950, a committee of three [from the Conference] met with top university officials. The meeting was distinguished chiefly for its brevity. After listening to a quick review of the program and work of the conference, Chancellor Robert Maynard Hutchins announced that he was going to have to do what he was frequently forced to do because of his busy schedule—make a statement of his own position and then leave for another appointment.

" 'He made an excellent declaration of principle on the race issue and began putting on his hat and coat,' said one of the committee members later."

(It was only after a change of administration that the University of Chicago eventually got involved to the extent of taking active leadership in community improvement.)

What were the results of the communication processes initiated and organized by the Hyde Park–Kenwood Conference? Mrs. Abrahamson tells some of the results by 1959:

"An increasing number of citizens now see deterioration, rather than the Negro, as the chief enemy. This realization came as they realized, with the in-migration of southern rural whites, that lack of urbanization created the same problems regardless of color and that the real difficulty was one of class. . . .

"A warm new spirit of kinship is abroad, the feeling that 'we are all in this together'. . . .

"The community of 1949, immobilized by fear and anxiety, lethargy and pessimism, is immobilized no longer. . . . Confidence and optimism are evident in conversations . . . in public meetings, in the fact that present residents have decided to remain, and in money invested in the area. . . .

"The Hyde Park–Kenwood Community Conference [is] now generally accepted as a potent force by all community interests. . . . The South East Chicago Commission . . . and an influential constituency adds urgently needed strength. . . . Most powerful ally is the University of Chicago with its great prestige and assets, now fully committed to community improvement and a leading factor in it. The churches and temples, the PTA's, the businessmen's associations, the *Hyde Park Herald,* the educational institutions and hospitals . . . are also involved in greater or lesser degree. So are Chicago's mayor, the community's two aldermen, every department of the city government, state and federal bodies—all putting tremendous resources into Hyde Park–Kenwood as Chicago's first urban renewal area."

Science has been the one field of human activity in which the sharing of perceptions of publicly confirmable evidence, the disciplined progress from lower to higher levels of abstraction, and the determination to build larger and more general agreements on a foundation of little agreements have been the rules for the organization of communication. In the work of the Hyde Park-Kenwood Community Conference, we have another, perhaps less systematic but no less genuine, application of a scientific, time-binding orientation to the clarification and solution of problems. Strato started discussion with an empty vessel and a basin of water; Hyde Parkers started with neighborhood deterioration and kitchenette apartments. Both systems of communication start with shared perceptions at the lowest levels of abstraction—and go on from there.

In a pluralistic society such as we have in America, we have learned, especially in our cities, how to get along with each other through the sharing of perceptions. Catholics and Protestants and Jews co-operate in our mixed societies by avoiding confronting each other with theological differences and sharing perceptions as members of the same teaching staff, office force, or bowling team. In a pluralistic world, nations get along together by respecting each other's cultural differences and co-operating on what might be called international housekeeping: the enforcement of international maritime regulations, agreement on postal exchange, treaties for the extradition of criminals, the creation of international systems of air-traffic control, and all the other minutiae of international discourse.

Sometimes people ask if it is not possible that some unscrupulous person possessing great knowledge of communicative processes through the study of general semantics might use that knowledge as a means of taking advantage of others. Such an outcome would seem to be hardly possible, because general semantics can involve no such separation of ends and means. In the general semantics theory of time-binding, the end is in the means, and means are all part of the end. The mutual enrichment that we derive from communication—my perceptions being corrected and enriched by yours, yours being corrected and enriched by mine—are the piece by piece realization of that communion among men that was dreamed of by the great men throughout the course of history who have been creating and improving systems of human co-operation and communication, from the builders of prehistoric burial mounds, to the founders of the great religions and great empires, to the creators of science and the scientific tradition.

Furthermore, the goal of the Stage of Shared Perceptions is not the triumph of one ideology over another, one world view over another. It is merely the establishment of enough shared perceptions among all people about commonplace things, such as food, shelter, housing, waterways, maritime law, fishing rights, tariffs and trade, and the necessity of slowing down the international armaments race, so that, even if we differ about larger and more abstract matters, we shall not have to go to war over these differences.

I have said that the one great task of general semantics is to advance time-binding. If enough people in enough places are enabled, through the study of general semantics or anything else, to acquire the orientations of science with respect to their most pressing problems, artistic, political, and ethical as well as scientific and technical, then a time may be envisioned when groups, classes, and even nations might begin to listen to each other with the specific intent of finding even small areas of agreement upon which larger agreements may eventually be built. If such a time ever arrives, it will not come simply because we desire it. It will come because enough people have disciplined themselves in the *avoidance of those orientations which inevitably lead to failures in communication and therefore to disagreement.* It is interesting to note that the training of counselors in the client-centered therapy of Carl Rogers can be described in general semantics terms as consisting in large part of training in the avoidance of just such orientations. In group dynamics, which can be described as small-scale time-binding, the training of group leaders is training of the same kind. No doubt there are other disciplines which have likewise found ways of making operative in everyday life the orientations of science. It is finally the task of general semantics, therefore, not only to promote time-binding in its own way, but to promote it by systematizing and disseminating knowledge of those rising psychological, biological, and social disciplines which are each, in their own way, increasing the total amount of time-binding in the world.

Le Roi Matthew - Pierre Smith